BCL

D1179860

THE PHILOSOPHY OF RELIGION

THE PHILOSOPHY OF RELIGION

RELIGION

from the standpoint of
Protestant Theology

By
EMIL BRUNNER

Translated by
A. J. D. FARRER
and
BERTRAM LEE WOOLF

JAMES CLARKE & CO. LTD.
33 STORE STREET   LONDON W.C.1

First Published in 1937
This Edition 1958

Made and printed in Great Britain for James Clarke & Co. Ltd. by
A. Wheaton & Co. Ltd. Exeter.

FOREWORD TO FIRST EDITION

The " Theology of Crisis " has affected theological thought profoundly during the last fifteen years, and has gone far to correct the liberalism that threatened to reduce Christianity to a mere humanism. Even among those scholars who have been as yet unable to accept it, its influence is at least noticeable, and sometimes further-reaching than they would perhaps care to admit. Up to the present, no systemic exposition of the underlying philosophy has been available in English, but the translation now offered of Dr. Emil Brunner's *Religionsphilosophie evangelischer Theologie* will, it is hoped, go far to supply the need.

The actual work of translating has been by no means easy, and our best thanks are due to Dr. Brunner's criticisms of our efforts to give an adequate rendering to his thought. We have been greatly assisted also in several difficult passages by Rev. Austin M. Farrer, M.A., Fellow of Trinity College, Oxford, who has had the advantage of sitting at Dr. Brunner's feet.

In order to make the book useful to a wider circle of readers, we have added to the original text a translation of most of the Greek and Latin quotations. On the other hand, we have not thought it necessary to reproduce Dr. Brunner's bibliographies which are almost entirely confined to works in German. It should also be remarked that he makes far larger use of inverted commas than is customary in English writers. We have thought it best as a rule to follow his method. Where the reason is not otherwise apparent, readers should assume that he is using words or phrases characteristic of some author or school that he has in mind at the moment.

We hope that the results of our efforts will enable many students of the philosophy of religion to come to closer grips with the " Theology of Crisis ", and particularly with the thought of the eminent author of the present volume.

A. J. D. F.
B. L. W.

NEW COLLEGE,
  UNIVERSITY OF LONDON.

CONTENTS

PART I : THE PROBLEM

CHAPTER I

THE MEANING OF PHILOSOPHY OF RELIGION FOR PROTESTANTISM

Philosophy consists in reflection on the connection between all particular facts, and the means it employs to this end is thought investigating the way in which the facts are intellectually founded. But we shall need first to supply the ground for the inquiry into connection by showing that the latter has intelligible meaning. Hence we must define the problem of philosophy more closely and say that it inquires how far a mental ground is discoverable for the connection between particular facts. By this means we shall become convinced of the necessity, and therefore of the justification, of the inquiry in itself irrespective of its subject matter. Such an inquiry, again, will include that into the meaning of all science, all civilization and indeed human life in general. But when any school of philosophy surveys the more significant expressions of human life, it will discover among them a form of life which on the one hand is in the closest connection with the set of problems peculiar to philosophy, while on the other it has characteristic differences from every school of philosophy, or is even actually opposed to philosophy. This form of life is religion. The kinship between the two rests on the fact that religion as well as philosophy has in view the whole of existence and life ;   the opposition between them consists in the fact that religion itself claims to supply an answer to the crucial question about reality. It gives this answer in the shape of revelation, and not as the result of the methodical reflection of the intellect, i.e. of an activity within the bounds of reason. Thus philosophy is brought face to face with a most difficult problem, that of showing the meaning and justification of religion within the mental ground known to philosophy. In this way philosophy of religion arises as a part, and perhaps indeed as the culminating point, of philosophy in general.

Provided, however, that the philosopher is serious in his concern about the truth of religion, he cannot avoid listening in the first place to the affirmations of religion about itself—and this always means the affirmations of some specific form of religion. It might of course be the case that religion will have to reject altogether any such classification under philosophy on the plea that it would involve a mis-interpretation of religion. In that case the relation between the two would have to be determined conversely, i.e. by starting from religion. Then religion would not have its basis assigned within the bounds of philosophy, but conversely, viz. philosophy, being a special department of man's activity as a reasonable creature, would take its place within the bounds of revealed truth. If such an assertion is not meant to forego every connection with the mind of science, civilization, and philosophy, we must of course make several requirements : that religion should find in her own presuppositions the grounds for thus inverting the relationship between ground and consequence ; that it should also report on its mode of supplying these grounds ; and once more, that, on the second presupposition, it should make plain the possibility of science, civilization, and philosophy. That would be the way in which, starting from the side of religion, the discussion would have to be carried on with a philosophy originating in the general cultural consciousness. But such an undertaking could be called philosophy of religion only in a secondary sense, and the name as just defined could merely serve to designate the sphere of the discussion.

The state of the case only becomes really clear when, as is incumbent upon us, we look from the stand-point of general possibilities at the special situation that faces us. There are two reasons why we can speak only in a secondary sense of a Christian, and more particularly of a Protestant, philosophy of religion. First, Christian faith, especially in the particular form given to it in Protestant theology, is a fundamentally different thing from every philosophy. To philosophize is to reflect on the mental grounds, with the assumption that ultimate validity belongs to the complex of grounds and consequences developed by natural reason. Christian faith on the other hand involves recognizing that this complex has been broken into by revelation. It is on this revelation that the affirmations of Christian faith are grounded. Theology, which is Christian faith in scientific form, could only lay claim to a scientific character provided it gave clear and exact expression to the fact that its complex of grounds and consequences differs from that of all other sciences as to the final authority it recognizes ; provided further that it developed all its affirmations purely out of its own presuppositions and thus founded them on that complex ; and provided finally, that on this basis it investigated the relations, whether positive or negative, between revealed faith and rational knowledge. Thus theology is on common ground with philosophy in showing the existence of an intelligible connection embracing all things ; but this is not, as it is for philosophy, the logos of the natural reasoning process, but the logos of revelation. Hence Christian theology can never be required to make faith rational by giving it scientific form ; on the contrary, it has to keep revelation and religion duly apart by means of clearly defined concepts.

It would be to weaken, or rather to do away with, the opposition were we to equate the relation between reason and revelation with that between rational and irrational. Revelation in the Christian sense stands in the same two-fold relation to the irrational as it does to the rational. The irrational (feeling, intuition, etc.) has not more but, on the contrary, less to do with the paradox of revelation than has the logos of reason. In the modern irrationalist philosophies of religion, the irrational is in every case grafted on a rational system (e.g. in the case of Otto and Scholz on an idealistic, and in that of James, on a naturalistic rationalism).

Neither can there be philosophy of religion in the strict sense of the term in the realm of Christian theology, for the further reason that theology has to do not with religion but with revelation. Whatever else religion may be, it is a mode of human life, whereas revelation is a self-disclosure of God. While the philosopher of religion is concerned with historical phenomena, i.e. with the historical religions and their "nature", the theologian is concerned with the ground of all phenomena.

To the philosopher as to the theologian, religion is not the ultimate fact but something that roots in the ultimate. In the former case it is reason that supplies the ultimate ground, while in the latter it is revelation. The aim of theology is thus something quite different from religion, and at bottom is no more closely related to religion than it is to any other department of human life. This conclusion, moreover, follows directly from the fundamental presupposition of theology : its ground, its content, and its standard alike are found not in any consciousness of man's, but in God's self-disclosure.

Christian faith, to which theology gives the form of scientific conceptions, is the knowledge and acknowledgment of God's self-revelation in Jesus Christ. He, the incarnate logos, is the ground, content, and standard of all the affirmations of faith. That is where faith differs from every religion as well as from every philosophy. By Christian faith is meant, not some universal truth, nor yet some universal religious experience, but a definite fact which as such is opposed to every universal, be it religion or philosophy. Not that it denies the existence of a certain universal knowledge of God, religious as well as philosophical : rather it presupposes this. But it does deny that the personal and living God can be generally known from possibilities that lie either in the world or in man's spirit as such. It contends that the living and personal God can be known only by a personal meeting, through His personal word, through that special event to which the Bible, and the Bible alone, bears witness, and the content of which is Jesus Christ. Hence this definite fact is not to be understood merely as an illustration, or an embodiment, or even a symbol ; where such language is used concerning this matter it is not Christian faith with which we have to do. On the contrary, the definite fact of revelation takes the place of what is universal, of truth in general, or of the final criterion of valid assertions ; the incarnate logos here occupies the position otherwise held by the logos of reason, the essential idea of truth. This is the case because the personal God, who is the ground of all truth, cannot be known as personal by means of idea, but only by personal, concrete revelation ; only when He no longer hides Himself, but issues forth and discloses Himself as the ground of all being, all values, and all thought.

This particular fact, this miracle of divine revelation, which by its very particularity is a stumbling block to thinking in universals, is the presupposition of Christian theology. Christian faith consists precisely in taking this peculiar view of ultimate truth. It would cease to be faith, it would indeed give the lie to its own affirmation, if it wanted to ground the truth of this affirmation on a universal truth. Either revelation supplies its own grounds or else it is not revelation. The only man who can look for some other foundation beside the *Deus dixit* is the man who withholds belief from the *Deus dixit* and wants secretly to replace revelation by symbol. Hence theology cannot substantiate its scientific character by such a change in the class of ground and consequent as falsifies faith, but on the contrary, only by giving a logically exact expression to this special, non-universal quality in all its uniqueness. But this means that theology is not a free science void of presuppositions, but one that is closely tied. It is tied to the definite fact of the revelation of God in Jesus Christ. How tied it is appears most clearly in the fact that theology is only possible within the borders of the Christian community or church, and has its definite content and its definite standard in the Bible. Only by perceiving in Scripture the utterance of God does a man become a believer ; and only as such, i.e. as a member of the community of believers, is the thinker in a position to think theologically. Theology is in place only in the church, just as in the same way its ground and content are to be found only in the Scriptural revelation.

This again is the starting point for a Protestant philosophy of religion, using this term now in the modified or secondary sense. Such a philosophy must come from theology and, further back still, from faith. It is not the case that it leads towards faith. It is a part of Christian theology as such, i.e. that part in which it carries on the discussion with the common consciousness of truth, i.e. with philosophy ; it is that chapter of Christian theology whose business is to start from definitely Christian presuppositions, and give a well-founded description of the relations between revelation and rational knowledge on the one hand, and between revelation and religion on the other. Hence it is not a universal science, of which Christian theology would form a subdivision as being the doctrine of a particular religion. This erroneous view was largely followed in the nineteenth

B

century. The very nature of revealed faith involves reversing the classification of universal and special in this case, because here a particular, viz. revelation, is regarded as ranking above every universal.

Despite the fact then that for us philosophy of religion can be only a branch of theology in general, we have good reason for separating it as a special science from theology ; the reason lies in the need of the times, which demands very special attention to this problem ; and the need of the times always has determined and always should determine the perspective of theology. Unlike the rest of theology, philosophy of religion is concerned with the formal and general problems of Christian faith, i.e. specifically with the complex of grounds and consequences set forth in the affirmations of faith as distinct from all other affirmations, in other words, with the problem of revelation. Nowhere, however, is it less possible than here to keep form and content apart : what is to be the Christian conception of revelation can only be made clear in connection with the content of that revelation. But it is at least possible to distinguish between form and content. On this distinction will depend the possibility of discussing the problems of philosophy of religion apart from those of theology proper. Such separation involves the further condition that, to a greater extent than in theology as such, philosophy of religion must have its being in the realm of abstract concepts, despite the fact that the conceptions have here just the same wholly concrete and personal basis as they have in the simplest confession of faith ever made by an unlettered man. At bottom, the philosopher of religion knows no more than any plain Christian : he merely knows it in the more exact form of abstract conceptions and in connection with the rational knowledge of his age. The reverse side of this advantage is that the abstract nature of his knowledge imperils the personal character of his faith—which ought to penetrate the said knowledge—even more than does the abstract nature of theology in general.

There is no fundamental difference between a theological and a non-theological expression of Christian faith. All utterance about God, no matter how much of personal earnestness it may have, has always the abstractness of theology. Even the parables of Jesus are theology. And conversely, the very earnestness of a personal, vital faith may lead it in certain circumstances, e.g. in its discussion and contention with the thought of one's age, to avail itself of the most abstract forms conceivable. Yet the primary interest of Christianity is not systematic knowledge, but the relation of a personal faith to revelation. Hence of course faith is constantly directed towards overcoming abstract concepts as completely as possible ; and therefore the philosophy of religion must be judged as lying at best on the edge of Christian doctrine and never at its centre.

Revelation meets and fits human consciousness. It is not a matter of indifference that this consciousness should be defined as human, although on the other hand it is not essential to know in what more specific way it is so defined. Faith is indeed bound up with humanity but not with any particular grade of humanity. Of course it presupposes man as man, but not a particular type of humanity, nor yet any particular feature in man. It takes man in his totality, not in some special locus that can be fixed by psychology. The locus in which revelation and the spirit of man meet each other cannot be assigned positively but only negatively : it consists in receptivity. If in place of this we would rather put a particular form of consciousness, we might say that it is " inquiry " when this has assumed the form of a vital need. But although this is a presupposition for faith, it does not designate a particular psychological quality, but, on the contrary, what is universally human. In fact, we can indicate the locus yet more definitely without thereby abandoning what is universally human : the negative point of contact is a consciousness of vital need which is at the same time a consciousness of guilt. Therefore we might fittingly express our meaning as follows : any account of the faith evoked by revelation should be preceded by another account giving the results of man's investigation of universal mental characteristics, which investigation would lead up to the afore-mentioned point of contact. Lack of space obliges us to omit such an account. Ultimately, however, this makes no difference because in every case faith appropriate to revelation must be understood entirely by itself and not by means of any common consciousness of man's. Faith appropriate to revelation can be understood only by revelation, just in the same way as any rational thought can only be understood by its ground in reason, or a sensation of light only by the light-stimulus. Therefore it is necessary to start from revelation as known to faith ; in doing so we have only to bear in mind that revelation is always the answer to a question on man's part. But whether man's question, and indeed humanity itself, have their ground in revelation, and only in it can attain their proper meaning ;   and therefore whether man's question has not its *prius* in God's address to him—these are matters that can be discussed only in connection with the knowledge appropriate to revelation. At all events faith is certain that revelation alone enables us rightly to apprehend that need, that vital incapacity, which is the presupposition of faith ; and that thereby revelation itself begets its own presupposition in the crucial sense.

Chapter 2

THE REFORMERS' DOCTRINE OF REVELATION AS A HISTORICAL STARTING-POINT

While Holy Scripture is the classical expression of Christian faith, neither it nor any parts of it can be claimed as the starting-point of our present inquiry, although this might at first sight have been expected. The Scriptures do not figure in Christian theology as " the religious views of the nations ", nor as a religious document, nor as the expression of faith, but as the ground and norm of faith. Hence they cannot serve as our starting-point but rather as our abiding standard of reference. As starting-point, as the pattern of a Christian knowledge of revelation, we may choose the Reformation confession of faith as being that expression of faith which, although outside the Bible, most clearly expresses the view that the faith founded on the Scriptures takes of itself. In the early church, thought about the basis of faith was concerned exclusively with its content, and this is in keeping with the nature of faith. Reflection on the formal problem of the norm had to find a beginning only when an understanding of the peculiarly Christian norm was seriously confused among Christians by alien ideas ; when a teaching having the continuity

of history was taking the place of a revelation given
once for all. This feature was seen in the doctrine of
the authority of the church and of a tradition which
ran parallel to the Scriptures and which was of equal
weight. The Reformation was a protest against this
calamitous transformation of the original Christian
principle of revelation, which was indissolubly connected with the uniqueness, the ἐφ᾽ ἅπαξ, the " once
for all " of the apostolic message. According to the
testimony of the apostles, what took place in Christ
took place once for all. There was no historical continuity of revelation but only a paradoxical unity
between that unique event and the present time,
the contemporaneity of faith with revelation which
is immediate and independent of intermediary criteria.
Between Christ as the mediator and the believer
there is no intermediation, because this could come
about only by means of a continually renewed incarnation of the logos, thus contradicting the apostolic
dictum " once for all ". Only God, as the Holy
Spirit, can speak again the word which was spoken
at that time once for all, and speak it in the heart of
the believer at any later moment in history. God as
identical with Himself in His historically unique revelation, and in the " subjective " knowledge that appro-
priates it, God as the ground, object, and subject of
knowledge, the triune God, is the content of Christian
faith, a content incomprehensible to reason. The
norm of that faith was formulated in the creed of the
early church. With it corresponds, as the doctrine
of the formal norm, the Reformation principle of
Scripture, viz. the word of God in Scripture which
is identical with the word of God in the soul,

or in brief, Scripture and spirit in their paradoxical and incomprehensible identity.

In this way the Christian normative principle is marked off on two sides : from realistic heteronomy or authority, and from idealistic autonomy or freedom. Realism makes us dependent on a given fact, and thus on something which, as itself relative, has a place in the flux of relative phenomena. At the same time, it makes us dependent upon something external which seems foreign to us. By the former dependence the bond is made uncertain, by the latter, " dark " or " blind ", because it does not take inward possession of the spirit. Hence a protest must be raised against it in the name of idealism. Idealism will recognize as binding only what comes from within and not what comes from without : accordingly what it recognizes cannot be a datum but must be a non-temporal entity located in the spirit itself and therefore to be found in oneself in advance. That is the nature of its extraordinarily significant principle of autonomy. But it overstrains freedom as surely as realism denies it. Idealism does not recognize any irrational element either in the sphere of knowledge or in that of the will, i.e. it recognizes neither the incomprehensible data of reality nor the fact of evil. If we deal seriously with the question of evil, the deepest ego is not identical with, but in contradiction to, its idea of itself. Therefore genuine freedom, which resolves the contradiction, cannot originate in the deepest ego as if it belonged to that ego, but must be bestowed on it as something foreign that is at the same time truly its own. That is the divine challenge, the word of God, by which at the same time we recognize our self-contradiction, sin, and by which we are adopted again into union with Himself, and thereby into the divine purpose. But this word does not arise from our deepest self ; it is not an innate truth which has merely to be aroused or discovered. Rather it must come to us as a datum from without, a word of revelation which subjects us to itself as authority and yet, at the same time, lays hold of our spirits inwardly as truth. It is the eternal word of truth as a concrete and personal entity, as an event in time ; the primordial word of the Creator which man lost and which as a consequence he has no longer at command ; which he cannot call back to himself as an *a priori* principle by any sort of " recollection " ; it is the initial word set forth as a new revelation but now revealed as the final word, the word of redemption.

It is as such an eternal fact given in time that this word is presented to us in Scripture. The meaning of the word is Jesus Christ. This " given " quality of His is the revelation in history, as a thing unique and complete. The word has been spoken. It is as this finished work that it is preserved in the canon of Scripture, by means of which revelation and general history are separated for the first time. The concreteness of the word, the fact of its having happened in space and time, is not accidental as in the case of general truths, but crucial. Only thereby does it become other than an idea : it becomes a given authoritative word of revelation, not discoverable by ourselves. It is as much the nature of revelation to occur once for all, as it is the nature of idea to be *semper et ubique*, i.e. general truth. The entire emphasis

rests on the perfect tense, *Deus dixit* (God hath said),
on the ἐφ' ἄπαξ (once for all) of the proclamation.
This perfect tense, however, is not a *perfectum
praeteritum*, but a *perfectum praesens*. That word of
the past speaks to-day. This wholly external thing—
the letter of Scripture—becomes an inner word, a
certainty, insight, confession. It has not merely the
form of what is authoritatively given, but at the same
time the opposite form of self-evident knowledge.
It does not require blind submission but takes the
spirit inwardly captive, despite the fact that it is the
opposite of a " general truth ". That is what the
Reformers call revelation, viz. the eternal as a datum
in time, the ideal as real, unattainable righteousness
as a genuine gift, the unapproachable truth of God as
knowledge bestowed. Here the material and formal
principles of the Reformers are both one : that God
condescends to man and addresses him—that is
gratia (grace)—it is the " justification " of sinners.
But it is also the revelation as given in Scripture alone,
both in one, just as it is authority and freedom in one.

This rationally incomprehensible unity of freedom and
authority, of heteronomy and autonomy, of what is given and
what is not given, is the hall-mark of the Reformers' conception
of faith and the Scriptures. " I must know it as certainly as
that three and two make five ; for it is as certain, and even
if all the councils said otherwise, I know they lie. What
convinces me in this matter ? Not any man, but only the
truth which is so completely certain that no one can deny it."
The word " of itself, without any respect of person, must
satisfy the heart, convince, and seize the man so that he is as
if imprisoned in it, feeling how true and just it is even if the
world, all the angels, all the princes of hell said otherwise :

indeed even if God Himself said otherwise." " You must decide the point for yourself, even at the price of your neck or your life ; that is why God must say in your heart, this is God's word, otherwise it is uncertain." " Therefore every single person must believe for himself that it is God's word, and that he would feel in himself that it is the truth, even if an angel from Heaven or the whole world preached the contrary " (Luther). " Scripture is accompanied by a perception of its own truth which is not less clear than the perception of white and black." Faith is a " *persuasio quae rationes non requirat* (a persuasion that needs no reasons) ", such a " *notitia in qua securius mens quiescit quam in ullis rationibus* (a knowledge on which the mind rests more securely than on any reasons) ". " Car l'écriture ne monstre pas moindre évidence de sa vérité que les choses blanches ou noires de leurs couleurs." " *Maneat ergo hoc fixum, quod spiritus sanctus intus docuit solide acquiescere in scriptura, et hanc quidem esse αὐτόπιστον neque demonstratione et rationibus subiici eam fas esse* (Let that then which the Holy Spirit has taught us inwardly remain certain, that we should rest whole-heartedly in the Scripture, and that this is its own evidence and not to be supported by proof or reason) " (Calvin). Nevertheless the truths of Scripture are the opposite of general truths which are clear *per se*, " the contrary of reason " (Luther) and only credible, because God's authority guarantees them. " Even if you had all the wisdom of the whole of Scripture and all reason, yet if it did not come or was not sent from God it would be nothing at all " (Luther). " *si hoc fule* (i.e. feel that it is truth) *tum adest spiritus sanctus, quia ista non fiunt ratione in corde humano, nec omnibus laboribus, sed per Christum adest qui fecit aliter sentire* (If I feel this—that it is truth— then is the Holy Spirit present, because such things are not wrought by reason in the human heart nor by any toil, but the Spirit is there through Christ, who caused my change of mind)." " If you are asked : How do you know it ? You should answer : I know it because I so hear it in the word and sacrament and absolution, and because the Holy Spirit says the very same in my heart, viz. that Christ became man for me, died, and rose again . . . i.e. it agrees with the Holy

Scripture, just as the Holy Spirit writes it in your heart "
(Luther).

This paradoxical, unthinkable unity constitutes the
Reformers' doctrine of Scripture. It is paradoxical
in its content : the eternal logos as personal life in
time, personal righteousness as a free gift, the revelation
of God's glory in the darkest place of history. It is
also paradoxical in form : what is most inward is
outward, eternal truth is nothing else than a given
and actual word to be accepted on authority, a letter,
" brute fact ", to use Hegel's terminology. Moreover,
these two contradictory pronouncements must not
only hold good side by side, but be recognized as one
and the same in faith. This cannot be brought to pass
in the forms of human thought. A matter of fact can
only be eternal truth when it is God Himself, and the
recognition of this fact can only be God's own self-
witness.

The word in Scripture, Christ, becomes the same
as the word in the heart, the Holy Spirit. When this
happens by way of answer to the question presented
by human life at the " point " where from the human
side there is only inquiry, we have what is called
faith.

Faith is a *firmus assensus quo Christus apprehenditur ita ut
Christus sit objectum fidei* (a firm assent whereby Christ is so
grasped as to become the object of faith) ; and now at last
follows the decisive step : *imo non objectum, sed ut ita dicam
in ipsa fide Christus adest* (" Nay, not object, but Christ is, so
to speak, present in the faith itself " Luther). *Non dubito quin
. . .* (Christus) *ita etiam nos substantiae participes faciat quo in
unam cum eo vitam coalescamus* (" I have no doubt that... (Christ)
so makes even us sharers in His nature that we unite in the

same life with Him " Calvin).   Faith is *insertio in Christum* (our insertion into Christ).

Where the self is no longer an autonomous subject, but is only the theatre ; no longer speaking for itself, but only a sounding-board for God's utterance ; where subjectivity is effaced by the truth, inasmuch as the latter does not merely permit itself to be apprehended, but itself apprehends :   there takes place what the Reformation teachers call the *testimonium spiritus sancti internum*, the activity of the Holy Spirit. Faith is distinguished from all other forms of cognition or recognition by being alone fully concrete. When I perceive, I implant the percept in the picture of the whole of perceived reality. Only by this implanting does it become truly certain. When I think, I implant a thought in the thought-continuum as such. Only thereby does the thought become truly certain. In each case, the implanting in the universal signifies a release of tension ; the demand on the single factor is weakened in favour of every other. But in the case of faith, we cease to implant in the universal ; here we can " rely " on nothing, on neither universal facts nor grounds. Hence, viewed from the standpoint of the " natural man " faith is foolhardy rashness, a leap in the dark. From the standpoint of faith itself, it is not rashness, but necessity ; not a leap, but a case of being drawn and carried along.   What from the human standpoint must be regarded as placing far too heavy a responsibility on the individual factor—a decision in an exaggerated and maximum degree—when viewed from the standpoint of faith as such, is not a decision but a free gift, not exaggerated activity but sheer

passivity.   Moreover, the inconceivable unity of
unheard-of rashness and calm resignation is part of
the paradox of faith.   God—man, Scripture—spirit,
the act of faith, and the gift of faith ;   these are the
constitutive elements of the Reformation conception
of revelation

CHAPTER 3

THE COLLAPSE OF THE PARADOX OF UNITY

Nothing can be more readily understood than that this paradox of unity, which can only be maintained as such by a supreme exertion of faith, was threatened with collapse even from the outset. Collapse in this case could only mean a disintegration into non-paradoxical " one-sided " half-truths. The history of the collapse and of the reactions to it, is the history of Protestant theology since the Reformation. Here we have the theological aspect of this period of history. It is obvious that it can be described in entirely different terms if we adopt a purely humanistic or materialistic standpoint. Nevertheless, it is incumbent on us not to give up the theological estimate, which at the same time, if valid, points to reality.

(a) ORTHODOXY

The change to the orthodox from the Reformers' conception of revelation took place so imperceptibly that, until a few years ago, the opinion prevailed fairly generally that the orthodox doctrine of Scripture was purely and simply the logical development of that of the Reformers, whereas it was sharply opposed to their doctrine. In the case of the Reformers, faith was the paradoxical unity of authority and freedom, submission to something given while at the same time it was self-evident knowledge. It could and must be so defined, because revelation and faith were understood concretely as phenomena of human life.

The content of Scripture is true, not because as a whole it is to be regarded as God's word, but because and to the extent that God meets me there and speaks : He attests Himself to me as present and " decides me " :   that is why we call Scripture the Word of God. The witness of the spirit is the same as the " clarity of God's word " (Zwingli). But in the fact that God's word is not the letter of the Bible as such, but only this letter as understood in the spirit, the further conclusion is involved that the identity between Scriptural word and God's word is indirect rather than direct. There is no such thing as revelation-in-itself, because revelation consists always of the fact that something is revealed to *me*. Revelation is not a thing, but an act of God, an event involving two parties ; it is a personal address. Hence the word of Scripture is not in itself the word of God but of man, just as the historical appearance of the God-man is in itself that of a man. The incognito of the purely human appearance is unmasked only by faith, by the testimony of the spirit which enables us to hear the word of God in the mere word of man. Only by becoming " clear " does it become the word of God, and if it does not become " clear " it is not the word of God.

Orthodoxy whether " Reformed ", i.e. of the school of Calvin and Zwingli, or Lutheran, gradually lost this insight of faith, and from the revelation of God in act made a book-Bible which was true in itself, and the divine authority of which stood absolutely fixed as a dogma of the church, as an axiomatic proposition, if we may use Sadeel's phrase.

The *principium ἀναπόδεικτον et αὐτόπιστον* is the *axioma :
scriptura sacra tota est θεόπνευστος* (Sadeel). *Homines qui
intra ecclesiae pomœria sunt, de scripturae auctoritate non quaerunt,
est enim principium* (Gerhard). *Scriptura sacra . . . per se . .
divina etiam ante et extra omnem usum. Non enim illa tantum,
quae fidem et salutem directe concernunt, sed quaecumque in
S. litteris inveniuntur, Dei verbum sunt* (Calov). ("The indemon-
strable and self-credible principle " is " the axiom that all Holy
Scripture is inspired of God " Sadeel.) (" Men who are inside
the precincts of the church raise no question about the authority
of Scripture, for it is a principle " Gerhard.) (" Holy Scripture
. . . is divine. . . in itself, even before and apart from any use
of it.   For not merely those things which directly concern
faith and salvation, but whatever is found in the sacred literature
is the word of God " Calov.)

Out of the paradoxical unity between the word of
Scripture and the word of the Spirit there grew a
causal relation as early as Melanchthon.   The divine
truth of Scripture was deduced from its effects.   Out
of the *testimonium spiritus sancti* there finally evolved
a principle that the proof of the truth of Scripture is
in its moral effect.

Just as we deduce the value of medicine from its effects,
*eodum modo experientia spiritualis, quae consistit partim in con-
tritione partim in vivificatione, est testimonium certitudinis doc-
trinae.*   (" In the same way the spiritual experience which
consists partly in contrition and partly in renewal of life is
evidence of the truth of the doctrine " Strigel.)   The belief
in Scripture is a syllogism.   The major premiss runs : everything spoken by God is true :   this is axiomatic.   The minor
premiss runs : *nostra (inquit Moyses et Prophetae) dicta sunt
Dei dicta.* This *minorem probamus, tum praesentibus miraculis
. . . tum et sequentibus eventibus poenarum . . . et aliis manifestis-
simis testimoniis* ("Our utterances (say Moses and the Prophets)
are God's utterances.   This minor premiss we prove alike

c

by miracles in the present and by subsequent retributions . . . and other most evident truths "). From this follows the conclusion : therefore the propositions of Scripture are true (Flacius). The certainty of Scriptural truth, the *testimonium internum Spiritus sancti* (" The internal witness of the Holy Spirit ") is identical with *efficacia sacrae scripturae*, the *vis effectiva*, the *effectus illuminationis, conversionis, renovationis et confirmationis* (" The efficacy of Holy Scripture, its effective power, the effects of enlightenment, conversion, renewal, and confirmation "). Accordingly the certainty of the truth of Scripture assumes the form of a *regressus demonstrativus*. *Ab effectu, qui est divinus et salutaris, regredimur ad probandum* ("An evidential regress. From an effect, which is divine and saving we refer back to the thing to be proved . . ." Hollaz).

Once the fatal step is taken of regarding Scripture as true in itself, as revelation in itself, it is obvious that this quality applies equally to every single part of Scripture down to the smallest detail. Atomism is necessarily bound up with the conception of revelation as a thing. Out of an address made by an act of God has grown a universal truth having the force of law. The dogma of verbal inspiration is involved not as the cause but as the consequence of the new unspiritual conception. The identity of the word of Scripture with the word of God has now changed from indirect to direct. Luther could say : Scripture is the cradle in which Christ lies, or : *si adversarii scripturam urserint contra Christum, urgemus Christum contra scripturam* (If our opponents allege Scripture against Christ, we allege Christ against Scripture). Accordingly, he made the freest application of criticism to the books of the Bible. But the later doctrine runs : *ipsamet verba et voces omnes ac singulas individualiter . . . spiritus sanctus inspiravit et dictavit* (" the Holy Spirit inspired and dictated ... the very sentences and all the words severally (Quenstedt). This means that Scripture is now a holy object, a fetish. The inspiration extends to the entire contents of Scripture. *Continentur in scriptura res historicæ, chronologicæ, astronomicæ, physicæ et politicæ, quæ, licet cognitu ad salutem non sint simpliciter necessariæ, sunt tamen divinitus revelatæ ... Non tantum sensus aut res significatæ, sed et voces tanquam signa rerum divinitus sunt inspiratæ* (" Scripture contains matters of history, chronology, geneaology, astronomy, physics, and politics, and although the knowledge of these may not be directly necessary to salvation, none the less they are matters of divine revelation ... Not merely the meaning, or the things signified, but the words, too, as signs of the things, are divinely inspired " Hollaz). This theory reaches its climax with the assertion that even the Hebrew vowel-points are divinely inspired, although they do not occur in the canonical text of the Jewish Bible. As opposed to this, we should call to mind Luther's free expressions regarding many books of the Old and New Testaments, or his declaration that the prophets " sometimes uttered prophecies about kings and the course of worldly things which these seldom fulfilled and which were often erroneous "; that even Isaiah " mixes many things together " ; that Chronicles is no more than a Jewish calendar ; and that in these matters the Books of Kings are more trustworthy than they. This freedom of Luther's ought not to be confused with the theory for which he has recently been censured by Karl Barth, to the effect that he founded revelation on a material principle that could be announced in advance (cf. further *infra*, p. 150). When orthodox theologians had changed revelation into an unspiritual datum, they believed themselves at last able to meet their opponents on level terms, viz. the Roman Church with its unambiguous visible authority, the fanatics with their unambiguous principle of the spirit, the rationalists with their unambiguous eternal truths of reason. As a matter of fact, however, this doctrine of revelation proved to be the death of faith, and the dogma of inspiration the very point on which orthodoxy quickly and finally came to grief.

(*b*) RATIONALISM

Reason did not permit itself to be held down by the dictates of orthodoxy. The era of the great achievements of natural science began. The cosmology of the Bible was shattered by Copernicus, Galilei, and Newton ; its chronology was rendered obsolete by a critical science of history and the imposing results of palæontology. Literary criticism of the Bible brought to light the thousands of contradictions and human characteristics with which the Old and New Testaments abound. In this way the authority of the Bible was completely overthrown. Should there still be such a thing as absolute divine truth, it could no more be sought in Scripture than in the hierarchical system of the Roman Church. All that remained untouched was the " eternal truths of reason ". On them rested the progress of science, on them, i.e. the *notiones communes* of Stoic popular philosophy, the Platonic ideas (somewhat transformed in a popular direction), it was thought that a satisfactory ethic, with a natural theology as its buttress, could be erected. In the first place, the Christian dogma of revelation was overturned and emptied of content by Socinian criticism in detail of specially objectionable dogmas and Bible passages ; then by thorough-going rationalism, until at last nothing was left of it except the three great ideas of the Enlightenment ; God, Freedom, and Immortality. But these again were exposed to every kind of exegetical caprice, to rationalistic doubt, and to an all-dissolving scepticism.

The last remnant of the Christian belief in revelation took refuge in the idea of God's gradual education of the human race. Here Lessing supplied the transition from the rationalism of the Enlightenment to the deeper reasoning of German idealism. Kant's critique of reason, principally his critique of moral and æsthetic reason, cut a path to the new view. The ground of reason, immanent in our thought and will, is the idea of God, indeed God Himself. Another idea united with this fundamental conception of idealism : that graded scale of all existences which Leibnitz recognized, treated as one spiritual nature which comes to clear expression by degrees, the teleology of reason that underlies all history. Taken together, these two conceptions led to a new conception of revelation which indeed might seem adapted to effect a synthesis between the Reformation and the Enlightenment.

The ground of all intellectual life is God Himself, and revelation is the gradually increasing consciousness of this ground that is accomplished in history. As the human spirit comes to itself, God at the same time discloses Himself, and this is His revelation in history. In Christianity, this truth is grasped, although only in mere picture thinking and therefore bound up with a concrete event. Absolute philosophy gives us the purified and completely intellectualized comprehension of this idea. It is a secondary question whether this mental basis is disclosed to us primarily in acts of will (Kant, Fichte), or of thought (Hegel), in feeling (Schleiermacher), or in intuition (Schelling). In any case, the point was that the opposition between reason and revelation was overcome by recognizing revelation in the power lodged from all eternity in the human spirit, of knowing its own spiritual ground in God. Every historical event becomes in this way necessary merely as a point of transition : historical events play at best the rôle of concretions of the universal idea, and these as instances or models for the individual person, can become the occasions of his own experience. But in themselves they never attain absolute significance.

That is the fundamental conception of the new doctrine of revelation as contributed by idealism. Starting pre-eminently from Herder, Hegel, and Schleiermacher, it penetrated and transformed Protestant theology. Systematically stated, the doctrine is as follows : the " place " and " nature " of religion is to be found in a general philosophy which is regarded as fundamental. In the general philosophy of religion the possible modifications of the universal nature of religion are deduced and historically illustrated. This philosophy shows how these modifications are determined by the varying clearness of religious consciousness (grades), and their varying relation to the other aspects of consciousness (modes). Finally the Christian religion is understood as the particular concrete example of the religious principle in history which approximates most closely to the idea (Hegel), or completely fulfills it (Schleiermacher).   In any case, however, the content, the essential element in religion, can be ascertained from the idea of the religion itself independently of any historical phenomenon, even if, in contrast to the Enlightenment, it be emphasized that religion must always have an individual form in history.

The problem of the general philosophy of religion is the question of the nature and truth of religion, i.e. its mooring in the universal ground of reason. Compared with this, the special theological question as to the particular content of the Christian religion is subordinate.   It follows that we must discuss even revelation primarily in general terms and without reference to anything definitely historical.   The historical has only the value of particular concrete examples ; it is only a symbol, a phenomenon of the universal, and as such the occasion of individual experience.   Genuine revelation, however, is precisely non-historical ;   always and everywhere identical, it consists in becoming conscious of the ultimate spiritual ground as this is lodged in spirit as such, and therefore also in the human spirit.   Revelation is an *anamnesis*, the last stage of an immanent recollection, an emergence into clear consciousness of what was always there.

God can only be known through God ; that is the fundamental thought common both to the idealistic and to the Christian doctrine of revelation. Biedermann was the most significant representative of logical, idealistic rationalism in the sphere of Protestant theology, and his doctrine of revelation was that it was " the act in which God makes Himself known to men . . . the *actus purus* of the absolute spirit in the life of the finite spirit, and indeed in a real interchange with finite, individual, spiritual acts of the human ego itself ". The decisive difference therefore consists in the fact that, for the idealist, the self-disclosure is fundamentally immediate, whereas for Christian faith it is fundamentally mediated. Granted that even Biedermann speaks of " mediation ", yet he only means thereby " the general psychic nature of mankind ". Hence faith is fundamentally independent of historical revelation. Jesus Christ is revelation only in a secondary sense—only as far as religiousness, i.e. the nature of religion, finds a stronger and purer expression in Him than in any other. This theory does not provide for any relation in the nature of authority, or an impartation of what is completely unknowable ; nor yet for any revelation made by definite means once for all, but only for releases of something universally and eternally present. The decisive Christian conception of revelation is excluded, viz. the disclosure of the divine mystery.

(c) Pietistic and Romantic Subjectivism

Squeezed in between rationalism and orthodoxy, and mediating between them at the same time as it was marked off from both, a place was made for a mode of understanding faith, the deepest roots of which must be sought in medieval mysticism. It was not, however, without important representatives in the Reformation period, e.g. in the person of Osiander, but it could assert its full influence only by way of reaction against the orthodox petrifaction of Biblical truth.

Pietism neither would nor could attempt the reconstruction of theology, because it consisted essentially in protests against the hypertrophy of theological concepts as found in orthodoxy. In the latter, interest was wholly directed to the question of the object, to the self-evidencing content of faith and the authority of Scripture. In Pietism, it was directed to the manner of appropriating salvation. Over against the catchword *fides quae creditur* (the faith that is believed) was set another, *fides qua creditur* (the faith whereby we believe). Once faith had been divided into two parts, into a content true in itself and the " appropriation " of this content, it was inevitable that a movement towards subjectivism should follow by way of reaction upon this false objectivism. Reflection was now occupied with religious *experience*, with the processes operated (!) by Scripture, the struggle of repentance, the process of conversion, the inward experience of love to Christ. But when once the main interest is fastened on subjective experience, the objective element, i.e. the Word, dwindles to a mere means of stimulus—for what matters is the " inward working ". Such experience of God or Christ becomes increasingly independent of any objective revelation in history. " Christ in us " became more important than " Christ for us ". Thus Pietism veers towards mysticism, i.e. to the form of subjective religion in which was sought an immediate experience of relation to God, a union of the soul with the ultimate divine principle apart from the help of word or other intermediary.

Protestant gnosis, as seen e.g. in Jacob Boehme or Oetinger, does not fall to be reviewed here. For it already presupposes faith and indeed the positive faith that answers to revelation. It affords not a basis for, but an extension of, the knowledge given in faith. The case is different with Schelling at a later date : his gnosis took its stand actually on Christian knowledge, but remained remarkably obscure as to its own origin. In his *Positive Philosophy*, Schelling meant to write entirely as a philosopher, and not at all as a theologian. Of course, he perceived it was impossible to reach the conception of a " living God " by way of philosophical reflection. He gave the name of " negative philosophy " to attempts of this kind which included all previous speculation in the realm of philosophy of religion. Schelling asserted, but failed to prove, that it was possible to set out from the conception of the " living God " without passing from the region of philosophy to that of faith and theology. But the working out of his system of gnosis goes to prove, on the contrary, that he himself needed the positive faith of Christianity for a basis if he were to be successful in passing from thence to his gnostic speculations (it must be granted that the latter do not lack significance for us to-day). A like uncertainty is perceptible also in Tillich's gnosis, which follows the lines of Schelling's. Here the ambiguous application of the conception of symbol makes it impossible for us to be clear whether revelation means a universal, an entity *semper et ubique* identical at bottom with itself, or, on the other hand, some definite, unique, and therefore decisive event.

Protestant mysticism was no more successful in reaching an independent formulation of theology or philosophy of religion than was Pietism in the stricter sense. But its chief current became an important factor in modern theology through its combination with motives derived from idealism and romanticism in Schleiermacher's theory of religion.

In essentials Schleiermacher's system of religious philosophy is that of idealism. But by a brilliant synthesis he fitted into

its framework the conception of religion that is characteristic
of Pietist mysticism. In his " Dialectic ", the general foundation
supplied by idealist speculation was employed to show that
feeling, i.e. pure subjectivity, was the " place " of religion.
In " feeling ", which is the point where willing and thinking
are still one, there is a disclosure of the Absolute, or the Divine.
Thus the most individual and subjective element of our nature
is the " place " where the principle behind the world is revealed.
At the point where there is neither will nor knowledge but
merely undefined feeling, lies the centre alike of the ego and
of religion. In that place, in feeling, the world principle and
the deeps of the soul become one. By being thus identified
with feeling, religion attains an independent standing as mystical
experience side by side with science (thought) and morality
(will). It is true that this is not mysticism in the pronounced
sense of Indian, Persian, Neoplatonic, or medieval mysticism.
For these give full scope to the thought that the Absolute is
reached by way of mystical experience. To the genuine mystic,
the world, culture, and society dwindle to insubstantial appearance. On the other hand, this modern mysticism is entirely
satisfied with being a " province in the heart ", in the sense
that the realm of objective reason keeps its independent place
side by side with it, nay even ranks both theoretically and
practically superior to this mystical experience. It is accordingly
a " mysticism " or " religion consonant with culture ".

Religion has thus won " its own " place in culture as a
whole. Its essence consists in an unmediated union with the
ultimate principle of the world. The unmediated character,
however, means not only fundamental independence of everything historical, but at the same time of everything conceptual.
Hence it figures in the rational whole as the domain of the
purely non-rational. It is only secondarily, i.e. through reflection
on feeling, that definite knowledge is, so to speak, admitted as
constituent within the pale of religion. But at bottom religion
has nothing to do with thought—not even with the thought
of God. The historical element comes into account here only
insofar as even this religion of feeling has a historical individuality
as living religion and can be aroused in others through historical

religious persons. The essence of religion is the same in every religion ; it is experience through feeling of unity with the universe, although always and everywhere it assumes a different individual expression and is capable of different degrees of clearness.

In essence, that is not only Schleiermacher's theory of religion, but also that of present-day neo-romanticism. It is the ground-plan of all modern philosophies of religion that pretend to recognize mystical experience as the essence both of religion and of revelation (Troeltsch, Otto, Scholz, Görland, and others). Of course, even mysticism is capable of a wealth of variations (cf. Otto's *Mysticism of East and West*) ; and of course, the speculative and the epistemological explanations of mystical experience are by no means the same (cf. the difference between Troeltsch (Otto) and Scholz, in their attitude to the *a priori* of religion). But in view of their fundamental opposition to faith founded on the Christian revelation, these differences from one another seem negligible. What is meant by Christian revelation has no place here, where the fundamental aim is an unmediated relation to the ultimate principle. The Christ-*faith* seems like " statutory dogmatic Christianity " in comparison with (Christ-) *mysticism*.

(*d*) HISTORICISM

Even in Romanticism an element had begun to make itself felt, which was bound violently to strain the subjectivism of the former and which broke away from it in the end. This element was the perception and appreciation of the place of history in its individual and non-derivative concreteness, i.e. the element of historical realization. Thence developed more and more decidedly the view that the really true and valuable thing is what is given us in historic fact. This view was related to Hegel's philosophy of history more in the way of opposition than of affinity. For

Hegel, the idea expressed in history was really everything, and the element of concrete realization as such was " mere matter of fact ", as indeed it is for any speculative idealist. That is why he thought he could conceive of history also, i.e. convert it into conceptions, by means of his nimble " dialectic ", and thus dissolve the oppositions inherent in it into the notion of the absolute idea as being mere dialectical modifications of the latter. The procedure of historical Positivism was quite different. It perceived that historical reality could not thus be dissolved away. Nay more : precisely in the element that resisted resolution into idea, it recognized at once the characteristic subject of history and the characteristic subject of value, i.e. the inexplicable individual element. It is against the background of this universal historical positivism that we must seek to understand that historicism, whether in the philosophy of religion or in theology, which constitutes the last phase of Protestant theology.

In the last phase of his development, Schleiermacher himself already followed this trend of the times and marked out the path for theologians who succeeded him. He recognized that his mystical subjectivism could not do justice to the essence of the Christian religion. Hence he tried to combine a historical element with it by representing that in the embodiment in concrete and individual fact the form supplied by the mere fact became more and more clearly a content which determined the religious consciousness. Not only *is* Christian religion a concrete historical phenomenon, like every other living thing, but a conscious reference to a historical factor is essential to it. In this case the factor is its historical origin in the historical personality of Jesus. This reference to a historical factor ends indeed by being regarded as the essential characteristic of Christian piety. Schleiermacher did not perceive that this carried with it not the completion, but the surrender, of the whole of his earlier and purely subjective conception of religion, the precise aim of which was to exclude all objective content. His doctrine of faith fluctuates between two conceptions of religion that are fundamentally irreconcilable: (1) That religion consists in a *feeling* of union with the Infinite that is void of any idea, and (2) that Christian religion is a conscious relation to the historical personality of Jesus of Nazareth, and accordingly it is *knowledge* of him, including the knowledge that he is the originator of the Christian religion. These two lines of thought are held together, but only seemingly so, by a third conception—that this significance belongs to Jesus, because in him the religious consciousness (understood in the sense of the first definition) finds expression in exemplary perfection, and hence he can redeem other men by arousing in them that same consciousness.

This relation to the historical person of Jesus takes on another form in the theology of Albrecht Ritschl through being founded not on the mystical, but Kant's ethical conception of religion. Jesus is the object of religious veneration, because in his person the ethical idea of loyalty to one's calling, or surrender to the general moral purpose of the universe, or the moral supremacy of human personality over nature, finds perfect expression. Because we recognize this peculiar moral significance in him, we " judge him to be God " as Ritschl's daring formula puts it. We have here, at least as far as intention goes, a return to the Reformers' conception of faith and revelation. Faith becomes a relation to a point in history : the person of Jesus becomes the revelation of God, and revelation means announcement of the will of God. Thus we cannot deny the intention here of renewing contact with the Reformers—an intention of which there is no trace in either Schleiermacher, or Hegel or Herder ; yet as little can we overlook, on the other hand, the fact that this contact, though intended, is not actually achieved. In the Reformers there is of course no thought that a historical personality as such, i.e. as a phenomenon in history, was capable of being " judged as God ", because that personality represents perfectly a moral idea. It is not with a " value-judgment " that they have to do, i.e. not with measurement by a moral ideal, but with a judgment of reality : we call Jesus God because he really is God. We call him the revelation of God because he announces to us what, apart from him and his announcement, cannot be known, i.e. God's mind toward us. He reveals that God, who is equally righteous and good, communicates to us that He is gracious to us sinful men and wills to bestow His life on us —a fact that could not be known apart from this communication. There is an unbridgeable gulf between this thought of the Reformers' and Ritschl's statement that " the ethical estimate of Christ which is based on his mission brings in its train the religious estimate of him as revelation ". That historical appearance which for the Reformers was the incognito of God in Jesus Christ is the revelation of God for Ritschl and his followers. The idealist foundation of Ritschl's thought betrays itself in the fact that what he calls revelation is merely the rendering concrete or actual of an idea that is also known apart from this historical manifestation. We must notice, however, in this case that the idea, the universal, in virtue of which " the estimate " is made, is the ethical idea.

But even if we disregard this ill-starred attachment to the Reformers, there still lurked in this historicism a discord which the further development of theology brought out with alarming clearness. The attempt was made to retain the Absolute in a historical phenomenon, but it proved impossible to fence it off from the relativity of historical phenomena as such. It is only the latest phase of theology, known as the " religious-historical ", which, in its most distinguished representative Troeltsch, has drawn out the consequences of historicism to the bitter end, and by so doing has done away with theology as such. It takes the modern secular conception of history seriously. History is an endless flux, a continuum, and hence, relativity. In history there are no self-existent entities that can be isolated out. There can be no history of salvation in the sense, so to speak, of a compact, self-contained and separate formation in the world's history, for the precise reason that history is a stream, a fluid, and not a solid. History means uninterrupted development, incessant becoming, change without halting places.   All historical phenomena are constantly passing over into one another, like the colours of the spectrum.   Hence even " Biblical history " is merely a phase of universal history, and the history of Israelite and Christian religion is only one wave in the great stream of the history of religion in general.   It is true that in this history there are peaks, but they are only relative and provisional.   It is true that there are individualities of inexplicable independence, and these are not merely personalities, but also peoples, epochs, circles of culture, historical systems of values, like e.g. the culture of the Mediterranean lands and that of Europe and America, in which are also included all forms of value and hence religions.   But this thought of individuality in history cannot avail to isolate an individual phenomenon as absolute, but, on the contrary, merely to make every historical phenomenon fundamentally relative, because, as individual, it is always limited and so under the necessity of being supplemented. Even the standards and ideas which count as absolute with us, and in virtue of which we form the conception of the Absolute, are in the same way only historically relative formations and therefore involved in constant change.   The " absolute character of Christianity " was not hurt either by Hegel's or Schleiermacher's or Kant's philosophy of religion, despite the fact that the conception of what could be regarded as Christian was reduced by them to a certified minimum.   But now this absolute character was radically called in question, or rather denied.   In this connection therefore it is only in a very modest sense that we can speak of revelation :   it is " that inward sentiment and certainty of both the whole of things and of its existence, which we call religious feeling or religious sentiment ". That is " revelation in the form which everyone can experience and to which everyone can testify ".   From this form, revelation in the sense of a special event differs in degree.   True, even in this secondary and loose sense, " revelation " is not unimportant :   " for the productive power of the individual is in need of constant stimulus."   And among religious stimulators the personality of Jesus is the supreme instance for the time being. Christianity " is not the sole revelation and redemption, but the supreme instance of the revelations and redemptions operating in the process of elevating mankind to God ". But this too holds good only provisionally, and is perhaps only right from our western point of view—such is the tenour of Troeltsch's latest definitions. Whither further development may lead no one can say, for even the laws of historical development which we may lay down would perhaps hold good only within the sphere of that special western type of historical individuality upon which they are founded.

In a historicism thus honestly and logically carried out, Protestant theology attained its final development. In it there is no longer any possibility of maintaining a specifically Christian consciousness of revelation. To perceive this is however to come in sight of the further question, how far we have any right to regard as formulations of the Christian faith, the various kinds of " Protestant theology " which are determined predominantly by idealism and the Enlightenment, in other words, those recent Protestant systems of theology in general that are founded on philosophy of religion. All of them, Ritschl no less than Schleiermacher, start from a general conception of religion and correspondingly from a general conception of revelation. They obviously construe the revelation in Christ as a specific or concrete expression of this general idea. But this very conception stands in the sharpest contradiction to the properly Christian conception as we have made acquaintance with it in the Reformers' conception of revelation, and as it is also explicitly as well as implicitly contained in the New Testament itself and, further, in the great Fathers of the Church, and again in the confession of popular Christianity. There can be no question that a theology for which the revelation in Christ is only an individual expression of religion in general, and for which accordingly there is merely a difference of degree between Hinduism, Buddhism, and the Bible revelation, can lay no claim to the title " Christian " in the classical sense of the word, although a personal faith of wholly diverse tendency may very often lie behind these theologies. The fundamental distinction between the faith that rests on the Christian revelation and all religion outside the circle of Biblical revelation is given us in the Christian conception of revelation itself. This is simply and classically expressed in the Apostolic word : " And in none other is there salvation : for neither is there any other name under heaven that is given among men wherein we must be saved." For Christian faith, revelation is indeed not a " universal ", not something to be experienced *semper et ubique* by everybody, but a unique, definite, concrete occurrence. Hence faith consists precisely in man's being bound to this definite occurrence. It follows that, properly speaking, Christian faith stands in irreconcilable opposition to the idealist conception of revelation which dominates recent Protestant theology. The radical form of historicism has the great merit of having made this opposition unmistakably clear and of having shown thereby that no theology proper is possible on that ground, but only a general science of religion ; there can be no Christian church, but only a religious club.

It would, however, give a false picture of the history of Protestant theology were we to fix our attention one-sidedly only upon the above-mentioned tendencies. The phases of development we have sketched are not self-contained entities, but only specially prominent traits which rise out of a general and scarcely definable background of a Christian ecclesiastical sort. But they attract special attention because in them we see at their sharpest the points in the discussion with intellectual life in general. But side by side with them there runs through all the centuries a theological activity of a more conservative tendency, which is nourished essentially on thoughts derived from the Bible, the universal church, and the Reformers. For contemporary consciousness, however, it is a less prominent matter, because it is but slightly involved in the intellectual conflict of any given time or, when it has been so involved, it has produced the impression of being an anxious, conservative, and apologetic defence. A philosophy of religion on a really noble scale, that thinks out modern problems in all serious-ness ; I mean, an attempt at an understanding between the Christian belief in revelation and the mind of our time is not to be found in that camp, with the single exception of *Sören Kierkegaard*. But as his thought is only just beginning to gain influence on the develop-ment of theology, this notable phenomenon will not be dealt with in our historical, but in our systematic section.

CHAPTER 4

THE PROBLEM PROPOSED BY HISTORY

If any meaning, i.e. any necessity, is to be discoverable in the course of development of Protestant theology, this necessity might best be understood by recognizing that there are four chief points of view to which justice must be done in any Christian doctrine of revelation : the relations between revelation and Scripture, revelation and reason, revelation and subjective experience, revelation and history. The one-sided prominence of any one of these points of view has determined the character of some one of the epochs in the history of man's spirit. But their one-sided prominence has carried with it the effect that one epoch has been displaced by another, and has led in the end to the dissolution of theology. Thus the task with which the Christian belief in revelation confronts us is to try to comprehend the meaning of revelation afresh in connection with all these four determining points of view at once, and at the same time with the problems of our own era. It goes without saying that it cannot be a matter of a " synthesis " of the said four tendencies, because you can never get a possibility out of four impossibilities by combining them. For the believer, again, it can never be a matter of allowing the age to dictate his conception of revelation. Such a theology would from the start be anything rather than Christian. No ! it can only be a matter of showing afresh, in clearest idea, what faith itself already comprises in the form of simple knowledge, viz. that a just conception of revelation is sufficient to take account of the interests of these four tendencies, provided that conception is consistently thorough. Further, our four chief points of view are not something foreign to faith, but arise out of it. We may take as proof of this the fact that the almost universal confession of Christian faith, the " Apostles' Creed ", lays bare the Christian faith on these four sides. It deals with creation and the " immanent " divine order lodged thereby in the world and men ; with the contingency of revelation in the historical phenomenon of Jesus Christ ; with the inward reception of the word by help of the Holy Spirit ; and with the historical character of the church, the community of faith. The mistake of isolating or giving a false independence to any one of these four " articles ", in other words, to one of the four chief phases of the truth of revelation, has occasioned the formation of one or other of the four mutually destructive historical epochs. It is the task of Christian theology to demonstrate their necessary interconnection by means of an understanding of the meaning of revelation itself. That is the only form of " apologetic " which it can practise with impunity and which cannot with impunity be omitted.

CHAPTER 5

THE ELEMENT OF TRUTH IN RATIONALISM : REVELATION AND REASON

In the abstract there are three possible relations between reason and faith appropriate to revelation : that faith finds a place in reason ; that reason finds a place in faith ; or that they are external to each other. The last could only mean a relation of irreconcilable opposition, the duality of truth which, however, if taken seriously would mean nothing less than the collapse of truth, for dual truth amounts to no truth at all. The first of the three " possibilities " is the fundamental thought of idealism. It attempts to deepen the conception of reason in such a way that even the truth of Christian revelation seems to be contained in it. To the extent that a theology accepts such a thought—we have seen to what an extent it took place in the last century—it ceases to be the expression of Christian faith. The Christian church has known from the very first that what she believes is a stumbling-block and foolishness from the point of view of rational thought. The object of faith is something which is absurd to reason, i.e. paradox; the hall-mark of logical inconsistency clings to all genuine pronouncements of faith. In all the periods when faith has been strong it has been the prime interest of theology to work out clearly the opposition of reason and revelation, of " natural " knowledge and will on the one hand and faith on the other hand, whereas conversely an apologetic attitude has characterized the eras poor in faith.

Yet it has always been the case that the believer shared at the same time in the general commonwealth of culture, and was bound by a thousand cords to the general mental life of his era, controlled as that life is by reason ; even in his faith, and especially in expressing his faith, he has not ceased to use reason. Hence, especially as a theologian, he owes himself and his contemporaries an account of the extent to which the opposition could exist alongside of the unity. His general solution has never been that revelation had its place within the bounds of reason, but rather that reason had its place within the bounds of revelation, because it is just from the standpoint of faith that the claim, but indeed also the limit, of reason could be understood. It is our first task to explain the nature of this mode of relationship which at first appears incomprehensible.

(*a*) The Problem of Knowledge, the Question of Genuine Reality

A naïve person believes that reality is simply there as a given fact. He is not aware what a vast fabric of thought lies stored up in his conceptions and images of what is " real ". We are reminded of it, perhaps, when we follow the laborious process of learning in a child, when we are faced directly with the primitive man's picture of the world, or when science shows that a difficult problem lies in what has apparently long been known. We " see " as a matter of fact a quite different world from that of a child or of man a few thousand years ago. Our heritage of thought is enshrined even in our " images ". Indeed the very fact that we make ourselves an " image " at all, i.e. that we take an objective view of the outside world, is by no means a matter of course, but an acquisition. On the other hand the progress of scientific knowledge which filters imperceptibly into our " normal " view of the world—I am thinking simply of the discoveries made by the microscope and the telescope—draws our attention to the fact that even in the present day our image of reality is very far from being complete. Once the question of genuine reality is raised it can never again be ignored. It is above all the self-contradiction involved in reality, when it is assumed to be " given " and observable, that makes it impossible for us to avoid research and thought upon genuine reality.

Every attempt at theoretic knowledge starts from the inner contradiction of the " given ". Therefore the driving force is the desire to overcome the contradiction and to establish the interconnection. An entirely single thing as such is not an object of knowledge. Indeed we can know nothing at all of an entirely single thing. What we always " see " is partial wholes, or things in connection with each other, but what we want to know is not merely things in connection so much as the connection of all things. We know that we have gained real knowledge only when we have made that discovery. The inquiry as to the connection is the inquiry into the " why ". But this question is ambiguous : it may mean either the cause or the ground. If we inquire for the cause, we are searching for an explanation. If we inquire for the ground, we are searching for understanding. In the first case we pass from one single thing to another, and we comprehend the whole, the connection, as the product or the interaction of the single elements. In the second case, we start from the thought of a whole in which the single element has its ground. The single element from which we began in the first case is " given ", it is a " something ". We soon notice, however, that nothing of that which we first described as single is really single. Rather it is already a composite thing, a relative whole. But we are looking for an ultimately single element in order thereby to explain the connection of all ultimately single elements. The whole, or the explicable connection, therefore, has its ground entirely in those ultimately single elements, and is not independent, but derivative. That is the fundamental conception of realism. But the ground from which we start in the second case cannot be a something, because a something can never be conceived except as a single thing. Rather the relation between ground and what is grounded is of an entirely different nature, viz. a matter of thought. Every thought which we think is a whole which cannot be resolved into parts. This whole is the meaning of a thought. The ground of a thought is always a whole of more comprehensive meaning. The ground of everything must, therefore, be the meaning of everything that has meaning, the thought of all thoughts, the truth of all truth. Employing the substantive used in Greek philosophy, I shall call it the logos. That is the fundamental thought of idealism.

Realism and idealism are possible forms of philosophy. They deal with the totality of existence. It is otherwise with science, which is neither idealistic nor realistic but always both at once. Its progress depends upon thinking. For it is only because a previous solution leaves thought unsatisfied that a newer and a better is sought. Hypotheses are only constructed by thought, and they constitute the real life of science. The contradiction in what is intuitively given only exists for thought, and thought alone can overcome the contradiction by analysis and synthesis. Science, however, does not trust to thought alone. She will have confirmed by experiment, i.e. the witness of the senses, what has been anticipated in the hypothesis. Of course, as she makes progress she increasingly resolves the manifold world, which is intuitively given at first, into connections by thought (laws of function). But at no point in her abstract activity can she dispense with experiment. Not that experiment of itself discovers what reality is ; rather that the hypothesis supplied by thought " says " something while experiment has, as it were, only to nod a " yes " or " no " to it. Experiment never says anything on its own account. It is only an indispensable control, the sign of a reality which cannot be completely resolved into conceptions, a criterion whether these conceptions are " right ". Inasfar as science makes progress she does it by virtue of these conceptions, but she is guided by the evidence of the senses. She is always rationalizing the reality given by intuition, and by her success she proves its rational nature. On the other hand the dependence upon the evidence of the senses shows that reality is not merely rational but rather an interpenetration of thought and of a datum which is other than thought.

The question is whether we can get beyond scientific knowledge, which is always confined within the finite and limited, and attain the final whole. Philosophy makes this attempt. For this purpose, the advantage obviously rests with idealism because when we pass beyond science we can only proceed further by means of thought. Every ascent, including that towards truth, bears testimony to the power of thought. Therefore we can understand that idealism proceeds to the bold assertion that, since the ground of all thoughts is itself the logos, i.e. the thought of all thoughts, and thus itself an idea and not a thing, so also that which is grounded and which we grasp by thought cannot be a thing. The reality with which we have to do is always that of thought.

Whenever we affirm truth, we are affirming a condition of relation to the ground. All truth is such in the truth, i.e. in the logos. Hence the true reality is the reality of ideas, and this again is the ground of our thought, and so too of our self. When we reflect upon our own ultimate ground, we come upon the ground of all being. The thought whereby we discern in the logos the ground of our own being is identical with that in which the logos itself enters into our thinking, and so with that in which the thought and the thinker are one.

Realism does not proceed so directly, for purely as realism it cannot bring itself to completion in a philosophy. Even for its completion, thought remains the only available means of constructing a philosophical system.   An elaboration of realism to systematic completeness is metaphysic.   Metaphysic starts from the scientific picture of reality, or, if you will, from reality as perceived by the senses, and completes its interpretation of being by means of ultimate hypotheses.   It follows that there is an indefinite number of metaphysical systems, in contrast with the thought of speculative idealism which is always the same in its fundamental characteristics.[1]   They have in common only a formal characteristic ; from a reality assumed to be known they derive by abstraction certain general laws, e.g. the Aristotelian graduated scale of various proportions between materiality and ideal form, and then by extension *per analogiam* (by analogy) of those laws they arrive at some final principles of being, e.g. Aristotle's *actus purus* (pure act) as the being of God—unless indeed they despair of reaching any ultimate interpretation at all.

But the mere fact that metaphysical systems are presented to us in such great variety that, on the other hand, certain great types of system, though frequently refuted since philosophy began, constantly reappear and obtain recognition, and that each of these great systems has just as many good grounds for as against it—all this shows that at this point we must consider how far we have here to do with knowledge.

[1] Despite the amalgamation of speculation and metaphysic that meets with such favour to-day (cf., e.g., Wust, *Die Auferstehung der Metaphysik*;   Heimsoeth, *Die sechs grossen Themen der abendländischen Metaphysik*), the sharp distinction I have made between them seems to me to be the view better justified both by the history of the discipline and its intrinsic character

Such consideration is the essence of the critical philosophy. Criticism starts from the nature of that knowledge which has the preferential claim to be called valid knowledge in virtue of its permanence and its capacity of winning general acceptance in the course of time, as well as by its practical utility. In it, however, we find side by side, as we have shown, a realist and an idealist element, not in equipoise, but in a qualitative relation of superiority and inferiority, such as is called for when hypothesis furnished by thought and confirmation supplied by the senses exist together. Now criticism shows by an analysis of knowledge that knowledge always consists of two features, it is both an elaboration of data, perceived by the senses and yet self-contradictory, into a harmonious co-ordination in thought, and also a limitation and control of such rationalizing by an X which is a datum that can never be resolved into a concept. Sense-perception without concept is blind, concept without sense-perception is empty. In its progress and aim, knowledge is rational, but it always has its occasion in an irrational datum that shows the way to the rationalization and sets permanent limits to it.

We do not mind if the perception of this irrational datum in its irrational and manifold character is called by some people " irrational knowledge " (cf., e.g., Müller-Freienfels, *Irrationalismus*, 1922). It is only a quarrel about words, whether, e.g., the disconnected perceptions of the senses are to be called " knowledge ". But it is not a rationalistic prejudice if we refuse to give the name of knowledge to an uncoordinated crowd of impressions. As soon, however, as order, connection, meaning, and significance enter into the confusion, the " logos " is at work. No end of confusion is brought into the discussion by inconsiderate use of the notion of intuition, by which term is very often understood the precise thing which is the chief feature of thought, viz. the understanding of wholes which are constituted by meaning.

The fact that we get at reality at all by an ordering process of thought is an indication to us of its rational character. But the fact that what we are able to set in order is never more than a certain "datum", the existence and nature of which always finally evades our comprehension, is an indication of its irrationality. Hence despite our knowledge we are ignorant of the true nature of reality. This twofold result is the quintessence of critical idealism.

Speculative or absolute idealism claims to know the true nature of reality, because it represents the rational or logos-element as solely true—everything is of the nature of idea. It believes that it can find the ultimate reality itself precisely in the idea of the logos without taking account of the fact that this idea is an empty abstraction lacking fullness of being, though not without a supreme significance. Speculative idealism does not perceive that our thought is always limited by the irrational datum, that it is just this limitation that is constitutive for knowledge, and that, just because speculative ideas lack this limitation, they cannot claim to be called knowledge. What they lack is "confirmation by experiment", i.e. the evidence of irrational reality. They are truth without reality, just as absorption in sense-data is reality without truth. It follows that speculative idealism, identifying as it does our idea of truth with truth itself, tends to be extravagant or visionary.

The relative opposition between the phenomenological and the Kantian schools of critical idealism can be disregarded in this connection. The objective character of the ideas, which is so strongly emphasized by the phenomenological school as against Kant, does not serve to transcend either the opposition between the empirical and the *a priori*, or that between the rational and irrational. The "philosophy which stands above all standpoints" is self-deception. Granting that the ideas are objective, there are still two considerations that cannot be denied : firstly, that they can only be known in connection with one another—and not, e.g., like stars in the sky that shine by their own light—so that to gain complete knowledge of them remains an endless task ; and secondly, that precisely for this reason there is no essential difference between discursive thinking and an intuitive view. Nay, discursive thinking never takes place independently of wholes supplied by " intuition ", while on the other hand ideal viewing—exemplified in Hüsserl's theory of " exclusion "—never signifies a datum pure and simple but always at the same time a laborious effort to appropriate it. Unless phenomenology advances to visionary speculation, as in the case of Scheler, it too cannot get beyond the " knowledge in difficulties " (Hartmann) which is exposed by critical idealism, and hence not beyond a fundamental dualism in knowledge.

A moderate speculative idealism made its way into theology through the agency of Augustine—called " Ontologism " ; its most pregnant expression is in the ontological proof of the existence of God. The nerve of it lies in the idea of truth. Since we are able to distinguish true from false, at least in idea, and since we know at least truth if not the Truth, it follows that we participate in the absolute truth, i.e. in God. It is only in God that we can distinguish between true and false, only in Him that we can think at all, or perform intellectual acts. For any such act is a μετέχειν τοῦ λόγου, a sharing in the logos. Of course this language of Augustine's can be used within the sphere of theology. But the critical thinker does not ask whether we can, but whether we must, think in this way ; whether on grounds of thought alone we are entitled to give the name of God to what lies as an eternal presupposition at the base of all thought. If the thinker gives a negative answer to this question, he agrees thereby with the Christian theologian, who would never recognize the God of faith in that idea of the logos or in Plato's thought of God. For this logos of reason comes short of divine being by lacking actual evidence, and hence reality, which after all is more than mere ideal truth. It is creation and revelation that separate the concrete from the speculative thought of God. Metaphysic of any kind is not less extravagant than speculative idealism from a strictly critical point of view. The strict man of science does not allow any hypothesis to count as knowledge if it is not confirmed by " experiment ", i.e. the evidence of the senses. But the hypotheses of metaphysic lack such confirmation. They are purely logical extensions or augmentations of the picture of the world as presented by science or even by naïve sense-perception. Their instruments are inference by causal regress and analogy, and these can never reach the unconditional and absolute, but only a maximum of the finite. The God attained by a metaphysic is never the Almighty but only a very powerful being, never the Creator but only a demiurge (*vide infra*, p. 85).

It is a false understanding of critical philosophy to think that it refuses any sort of justification to speculation or metaphysic. It only serves to show that these cannot have anything to do with real knowledge. Metaphysic originates in an æsthetic craving, viz. for a coherent view of the world, for a complete fabric of thought. It is really a product of the βίος θεωρητικός or life of contemplation, which is not the Aristotelian ideal for nothing. Critical philosophy, however, does not end with such a harmonious and satisfying conclusion, but with a very dissatisfying and deeply disturbing embarrassment of knowledge, i.e. with an open question, though not, as is often asserted, with scepticism or agnosticism. It knows too much of an absolute logos to be sceptical. But at the same time it is conscious of knowing too little of that logos to be capable of becoming " theology ". The real logos would have to be one in which the irrational datum could also be known to have its ground. But this ground is not accessible to our knowledge. The ultimate fact that we can know is that our knowledge is limited. For our knowledge, the Absolute is no more—though also no less—than a necessary limiting conception. Thus when we reflect on knowledge we are brought face to face with the question of the Absolute without however being able to give ourselves any answer to it.

It is a striking fact that in the discussion of the attitude of critical philosophy to the problem of metaphysic, very little attention is paid to Kant's *Critique of Judgment*. Were this otherwise it would be seen that Kant's conception of nature is not so one-sidedly causal and averse to a teleological conception, and that his perception of the traces of divine purpose in history is not so slight as is usually represented. Kant does not mistake the truth that lies in Aristotle's thought of entelechy. Indeed he pays high respect to the teleological proof of God's existence in the *Critique of Pure Reason*. But equally noteworthy is what he certainly omits to do : he does not trust himself to erect upon it a solid fabric of metaphysical knowledge. He knows too that this negative position is not merely negative ; it is intended at the same time to make room for faith. It is another question whether what Kant calls faith really is faith, but in any case he agrees with the Reformers in setting only a very limited value on *theologia naturalis*. They did not deny that a certain knowledge of God could be derived from nature. None the less, they laid all the emphasis on the wholly uncertain and insufficient character of any knowledge that was independent of revelation. This Aristotelian metaphysic should not be confused with the Old Testament belief about creation, for the former has to do with merely theoretical knowledge, the latter with faith. For Kant's *opus postumum*, on which an undue value is perhaps set to-day, *vide infra*, p. 71.

(*b*) The Moral Problem, or the Search for Actual Truth

Theoretic knowledge does not afford the only possible relation to reality. All theory is a matter of standpoint, and as "theoretists" we are like "spectators"

in a " theatre ". It may indeed be the case that the
reality which is presented to the spectator simply
cannot be the true reality, and thus that appearance
(theory) and actual reality are mutually exclusive.
Theoretic knowledge is not everything. It is a part
of life, but we are more than our theoretic knowledge.
For we are concerned with reality not merely as
spectators, but also as actors. Theoretic activity is
only a part of our total activity : and hence the question
of activity in general, or the practical question, takes
precedence of the question of theoretic knowledge.
The question as to the meaning of theoretic knowledge
is only part of the larger question as to the meaning
of life in general. We are living beings : but the
question is, whether the life we live purely of ourselves
is the true life. Reason gives a negative answer to
this question. We do not become men till we pass from
the natural life (into which we are born) with its
character as an immediate datum, and begin to inquire
about the true life, the truly significant and good life,
which is not a datum. In so doing we no longer reflect
upon the objective world, but turn to the acting ego
and ask : How do I become truly a man ? This
question itself implies a provisional answer, viz. that
the true ego is not a datum, but a mandatum or task.
It is realized only by acts of self-determination, when
we come into relation with the true ego. How the
true becomes the actual ego is the problem of ethics.
In this context the word " idea " has a meaning
different from and more weighty than that which it
has in the realm of theory. It is no longer an " on-
look " but a challenge. I am no longer merely a
spectator who may or may not look out on the world-

order, and to whom, therefore, that order is merely a hypothetical law. I am now personally concerned and challenged to a decision. Obedience is involved if the acting ego must be conditioned by ideas. The moral idea is an imperative.

What, however, is this idea ? Primarily it is only and solely self-determination. This looks like a purely formal definition, but it means an advance from the datum, the natural animal (*homo*) to man in the proper sense (*humanus*). The seemingly formal thought of a demanded self-determination really has an inexhaustible content : it is the thought at once of freedom and of responsibility. What I am thinking of is not simply my own responsibilities but those of men in general. The " thou shalt " that expresses my duty implies thereby the duty of every other man. The fact that this obligation is purely formal, defining form rather than content, is not a defect, but rather a distinctive virtue of ethics : it ought to lay the stress on form rather than content, on mental disposition rather than material result.

From this standpoint it seems possible to solve even the problem of true reality. Should not the true reality lie behind this idea of obligation ? It comprises indeed not only the ground of what we ought to do, but also the mental ground of knowledge. In the good the true also has its root. The good, as Plato tells us, is the queen of all the ideas. It is the pledge of a higher reality : by saying " you ought " it gives me a place in the *mundus intelligibilis*, in the realm of ends. And the realm of ends is only a "realm", i.e. a unity, through being constituted by a will, which is not mine but above me. It is the divine will, that challenges me in the law of obligation, and thereby raises me at last to the level of man. Does not this solution of the moral problem give us at the same time that of the problem of the universe ? For we know after all that the basis of everything, the logos, the idea of all ideas, is the divinely good will.

It is at this point that critical idealism becomes transcendental and speculative. We must show that even in this case logical consideration can only end in ἀπορία (perplexity). Firstly, despite every argument which is rightly brought to combat the objection that the ethic of critical idealism is not merely formal—or which maintains that any philosophical ethic formulating specific injunctions ties man to a content and thus degrades him from an end in himself to a means—yet it remains a defect of this ethical system that it cannot point out exactly what is the nature of human duty. While it is true that no attempt to give a philosophical answer to this question has been able to withstand critical analysis, this only means it is obvious that the difficulty cannot be resolved by philosophy. It is undeniable that even Kant had to borrow from the Eudemonism he had rejected before he could approach the problem of the nature of conduct. His ethic describes correctly enough the form of a good will, but from its own principles it cannot logically deduce concrete forms of action. Its law is universal, its ego is universal, and both are out of all relation to a specific case, and give no direction as to what is to be preferred or rejected in any particular instance. Secondly, the ethic of the critical school may describe the form of a good will, may know the idea of it ; but what about its reality ? Is the idea of the good will realized anywhere ? Of the critical philosophers, Kant is the only one that has seriously faced this question. It leads him to a remarkably ambiguous answer, or rather to two answers. In the first, it leads him to making a distinction between the actual man, who is fettered by the world, bound and determined by outside causes, on the one hand, and on the other the rational intelligible will, which is completely free, and indeed identical with the idea of the good. But what of the actual man, the man who should indeed do the good and knows he should, but does not do it ?

This question Kant answers in a second line of thought, supplied by his idea of radical evil. He acknowledges as a fact the strange phenomenon of the contradiction between will and law. Evil is not simply absence of good ; it is neither weakness nor sensuousness, but a positive quantity, the contradiction between will and law. This line of thought is so contradictory to the former that philosophers have commonly taken the view that it should be disregarded as alien to Kant's mode of thought—and indeed to philosophy in general. None the less, they both arise out of the central conception of Kant's philosophy, viz. his doctrine of autonomy. If moral autonomy is a fact, the law is our own law, and therefore our deepest ego is at one with the law ; it is itself the lawgiver, the intelligible ego. On the other hand, if autonomy is a fact, then where there is want of conformity with the law, the responsibility lies in the deepest ego, the rational ego, the αὐτός, and it alone. For reason alone is capable of responsible action. Only from a rational ego can evil spring. But such evil is not a chance product : it is a determination of the whole will, since the will is indivisible. It follows that the αὐτός, the responsible ego as a whole, is guilty of the evil, nay is so fettered by evil that it can do naught in all its willing but at the same time will evil. Thus our deepest ego is in contradiction with the law. One theory issues in doing away with evil, the other in doing away with autonomy. Nor is there any way of avoiding this contradiction. And since both lines of thought express realities in the life of the ego, the contradiction is not merely an impasse of thought, but a danger to life, and that of the most serious kind, viz. the cleavage of the ego at its centre.

Thirdly, we have to ask, in the last place, by what right is the idea equated with genuine reality in this case ? The only possible answer is that this equation is no less extravagant than that in the theoretical sphere. The moral idea of the good is no more God than is the theoretic idea of the true. Even moral thinking is a monologue ; this is another case where we do not reach a real dialogue ; a genuine non-rational self-witness does not come from the second party. The idea of the good is just as " empty "— though it does not on that account fall short of the highest importance—as the theoretic idea of the logos, because it also is only reached by reflection of a rational character. The identification of the moral idea with God is speculative idealism, or, as it is often called, in Fichte's phrase, " ethical mysticism." The idea of God drawn from practical reason is not God, but simply the idea of God.

Kant's struggle with this difficulty arrests our attention especially in his *opus postumum*. Nowhere else does the difference between Kant's faith and his philosophy come out so clearly.

At the same time, we perceive the steadfastness with which his thought opposes any other than a rational faith—which indeed is no faith at all. Kant as thinker knows that no idea of God has reality, not even the moral idea. On the other hand he is perfectly certain of the existence of God independently of human thought. And so he vacillates between the two, and this vacillation, his hesitation on the crucial question, is the most salient feature of this posthumous work. "The naked idea of Him is without more ado a proof of His existence." Yet on the other hand, he says " The existence of such a being cannot be denied, but neither can it be asserted apart from man as a rational thinker ".

The third line of thought has now to be brought into connection with the second : either the moral law is God's law (in which case we are not autonomous, not lawgivers, not even co-lawgivers), or the moral law is really a law given by ourselves, and the intelligible ego is our own deepest ego, in which case we have no serious knowledge of either evil or God. It appears then that the problem of evil is the critical point for the critical school of thought, the turning-point between a rational reflection on oneself and something wholly different.[1] If there is such a thing as guilt, if radical evil really exists, then God stands with His will over against our will, in fact in opposition to it. If, again, God is not identical with the ground of the moral consciousness inherent within us, neither can we have any knowledge of Him by reflection on ourselves, by mere exercise of reason. A real and personal God must meet us personally, must really address us by acts having the concrete, contingent character of reality ; that is to say, by an incomprehensible revela-

[1] Cf. the parallel shown by Tillich, in *Mystik und Schuldbewusstsein* (1912), to the critical turning-point in Schelling's philosophy.

tion, if we are to know Him as a real and personal being. This becomes specially clear when evil is characterized as guilt. It is at this point that the ἀπορία becomes a danger to our innermost existence, from which there can be no deliverance arising from within us, i.e. from the idea, or from thought analysing itself. For in this case deliverance can only mean forgiveness. But forgiveness inferred from the idea of God, forgiveness as something necessarily connected with the idea of God, is nothing short of the well-known blasphemy of Voltaire : *dieu pardonnera, c'est son métier*. This takes all seriousness from guilt. If, however, forgiveness cannot be regarded as a matter of necessity—and only what is necessary is certain in thought—it must really be *given* if there is to be any forgiveness at all, imparted in a contingent and non-rational manner. In other words, it must be revealed. It follows that the decisive question is, faith or man's reflection on himself, revelation of God or idea of God. Thus the problem of guilt and forgiveness takes the central place in evangelical preaching. Reflection on the self conducts us to this point, but if left to itself, must always lead us away from it again. Evil and guilt can only be seriously spoken of as realities on the ground of revelation.

(c) THE REVELATION OF GOD'S RIGHTEOUSNESS AND FAITH

Reason is competent to mark out the bounds of what can be the object of thought. But our knowledge of the existence of the non-rational as a limiting conception shows reason that in so doing it does not include reality in itself. It cannot know the nature of that particular logos which is not merely idea, but includes a non-rational datum, and, when critically exercised, reason knows that it cannot know it. Accordingly it knows that it can form no conception of God as real and personal, i.e. as the " living God ". Judged then from the standpoint of reason, the assertion of a real revelation of God may cover the purest nonsense or empty " visionariness " (Kant) just as much as the greatest truth. Wherever human limitations, superstition, or fancifulness comes forward with a claim to be revelation, reason is the censor whose office it is to unmask their true character and rebut them. The judgment of reason, says Luther, is reliable as to negative conclusions : but (so he continues) as to positive it is deceptive (he means, in reference to the assertions of theology). It cannot of itself find a way out of that ἀπορία, which, being guilt by nature, is a danger to life, a cleavage of the ego at its centre. It can only say that, if there were a way out, it would have to be an inconceivable, unthinkable event, the possibility of which, if it cannot be denied, at least cannot be comprehended. It can indeed go further: it can say that such a solution could only come about if that logos were to confront us as a concrete reality. But it simply cannot conceive of itself under this head. Revelation, if there is such a thing, cannot be known by thought, but only believed. And it *can* be believed only when it exists. Reflection cannot carry us beyond this hypothetical position ; the only thing that can carry us beyond it is that verdict given by faith which is identical with the miracle of revelation.

It follows that it can be no concern of our present

discussion to prove the fact of revelation and so to decide the verdict. All that can be done here is to show that only when revelation and faith are presupposed, and then in the sense in which they form the content of the Bible, can we speak of an " answer " to the " question " of a removal of that threat to existence. This then is not to be understood in a universal sense, as an inference from the nature of reason or religion, but simply as resting on a fact which only on the verdict of faith can be understood to mean a meeting of God Himself with us. It comes to the same meaning when we say that this is the only way in which we can speak of God at all. If God is anything more than idea, if He is a personal spiritual reality, we can only have personal knowledge of Him by His actually speaking to us, which is quite a different matter from the mono-logue of thought reflecting on itself. Assuming that He is a self, an ego, He must proclaim Himself as such to us if we are to know Him as such at all. He must Himself " name His Name to us ". For the " name " that we ourselves give to Him is not *His* name. What we think of God belongs to us. Even in the case of a fellow man we can only realize him as real when he does not merely let us think about him, but communicates himself to us by speech ; how much more are we referred to an actual communica-tion, if we are to know God, who is not indeed fellow-God, does not belong to our category, but is sole God. We cannot speak with a God who is merely the object of our thought. We cannot know in His absoluteness and reality a God who exists merely in our thought.

Neither does the moral imperative of Kant afford an escape from this loneliness of the ego (Ebner). It also has its being entirely in the silence of a dialogue with oneself. This is the reason why such morality does not reach a truly personal relationship. It is not, as the name " imperative " pretends, a genuine act of command, but a universal law. It does not provide the foundation for a personal relationship, because it is abstract—on one side is a neuter, viz. law, on the other side another neuter, viz. mankind in general. There can only be personal relationship where we are personally addressed. The universality of the idea makes it abstract and unreal. What we commonly call " reality ", viz. something concrete, is as such non-spiritual and untrue. True reality is present only in revelation—the Absolute as personal reality—the " logos in the flesh ".

The fact is that Kant's conception of personality is not truly personal, although it comes nearer than any other philosophical conception to the truly personal—incomparably nearer than, say, that of the individualism of the Romantic school. This is made particularly clear when Kant speaks of man or personality in a purely ideal sense, without any reference to sin, even where he is concerned with ethical conduct. Thus, to use Christian terminology, he puts unfallen in the place of fallen man, or the idea of man in the place of the actual man, not merely with a view to standardizing and judging the actual man, but above all to secure thereby a possibility of a self-redemption, such as is worked out especially in his *Religion innerhalb*, etc. The idea of man still remains the deepest and innermost centre of the actual man, and hence the putting forward of this idea avails to make man really good. It is on this conception of personality that Kant's phrase, " Thou canst, for thou oughtest," is founded, and this marks the point of his most extreme opposition to Christian faith.

But it is not only God who is unreal to us apart from revelation, but ourselves also. So long as we know ourselves only by reflecting on ourselves, we have no real knowledge of ourselves. The judgment we form of ourselves is either realistic and cynical, or idealistic and illusionary. Apart from faith, even in the most serious exercise of our moral consciousness, we see ourselves in the artificial illumination of autonomy as free beings who can do the good because they ought. This ascribes to us a worth which we lost long ago. We have no true perception of ourselves in the moral law, because we view ourselves *sub specie ideae*, i.e. in the universal idea, not in our concrete reality. Suppose we do notice an element of radical evil—and this thought of Kant's represents the maximum of self-knowledge accessible within the circle of immanentist thought, and therefore is rejected by most of his contemporaries and admirers—this thought has to be immediately suppressed again, because it upsets autonomy and the principle of immanence or knowledge by reflection on the self. To acknowledge oneself evil would mean to see a cleavage in the inmost centre of personality, and this we cannot do of ourselves. We lack the standing from which it could be done. Even if we were sinners, we cannot know this of ourselves. For sin is severance from the truth. But in order to perceive this severance or fall we must still be in the truth.

The man who has lost innocence can no longer appreciate what the loss of it means. To know whence we have fallen we must be able to see our original " place " still, or to see it again. Accordingly the testimony of faith is that knowledge of sin coincides with the miracle of the reinstatement of the lost, i.e. the " justification of the sinner ".

Knowledge of sin is possible only " in the presence of God ".[1] Thus we really know ourselves only when we really know God. It follows that the witness of Christian faith indicates a single point as the place where real God meets real man ; where man becomes real to himself, because God becomes real to him ; and this takes place here because in meeting with God he recovers not only God but also what was lost. That *one* point is the Cross of Christ. This incomprehensible fact is the place where the incomprehensible aspect of actual man, the revelation of sin, meets the incomprehensible aspect of God, the mystery of reconciliation. True reality is disclosed to us, and bestowed on us as real truth, as " righteousness ", at the point where our untrue reality is unmasked. Where " idea " and " experience " are farthest apart, or rather, where they contradict each other as divine decree and human actuality, the eternal logos is also present as a reality in the mystery of revelation, which is likewise the mystery of reconciliation. At that point truth is given as reality.

But what does " giving " mean in this case ? Where it is merely a case of giving, we are simply natural creatures, quite passively handed over to receive an impression like a receptacle or inert mass. What is spiritual cannot really be " given " to us. Hence Socrates, as depicted by Plato, designates a teacher like himself as the midwife of knowledge. True knowing is an activity of the self. Judgment and decision are required on our own part, and what is " given " is merely occasion for this, and therefore the communication is indirect. But the more indirect,

[1] Cf. Kierkegaard, *Die Krankheit zum Tode*, 73-129.

the more spiritual it is. With respect to revelation, however, we are neither passive as nature, nor active as spirit. Revelation is not a datum in the natural order, but is logos, meaning, word. Yet even this meaning is really given ; for we are not summoned to pass judgment ourselves or to verification by self-contained logical or ethical standards. We cannot "judge Jesus to be God ". By what standard are we to test the nature of the mystery of God ? How should we have within ourselves the standard of testing whether God forgives us, whether He wills to bestow His life on us in some incomprehensible manner ? We have simply to accept—or reject—this logos, this word as His " good pleasure ", His authoritative word. We can neither experience nor understand divine revelation, but simply believe it. Faith is the form of reception with our whole personal being as distinguished from a receptivity that attaches to nature or the spontaneity of the realm of ideas. But at the same time, it is decision of the most personal kind. Faith is the plain answer that we return when God addresses us—I believe and obey. Faith is the incomprehensible miracle of being able to say this only because God bears witness to the thing itself in us as the truth and guarantees it by His authority, the miracle that He Himself says Yes in us.

(d) REVELATION AND THE PROBLEMS OF REASON

The time-honoured opposition between idealism and realism is insoluble on the ground of reason or philosophy. For idealism, while it has the claim to superior truth because starting from the possibility of knowledge as such, always comes to grief on the concrete character of what is actually given, because this last can never be resolved into concepts, i.e. into universal ideas. Realism on the other hand, which constantly derives from this fact its power to withstand its superior opponent, also constantly comes to grief over the impossible task of finding a self-subsistent entity out of connection with the unity of thought, when such " finding " always means adoption into the unity of consciousness. The realist is not aware how much of " idealism " lurks in the mere search for knowledge. Critical idealism can indeed ultimately point out this dualism in knowledge, but not overcome it. It can show that any would-be definite solution of the problem of knowledge is probably illicit, but just for that reason it cannot itself supply one. What if the solution were impossible for the reason that the question was wrongly stated, or rather, because in both cases the answer was looked for in a wrong direction ?

Idealism and realism alike are in search of a theoretic and objective solution of the problem of knowledge, i.e. both seek indubitable reality. But we may ask : What if true reality be not anything " objective " in this sense at all, because it is something personal ? If we start from the common consciousness and behaviour of men, the question naturally suggests itself in regard to the artificial attitude of aloofness from the world which is presupposed in " objectively theoretic " knowledge—does that attitude achieve the manifest gain which it secures at the cost of a less manifest, but all the more far-reaching, loss ? We need not hold mere lack of the power of abstraction or deficiency in scientific capacity responsible for the fact that great nations as wholes or even civilizations have no acquaintance with the problem of science or philosophy, or with rational inquiry in general ; or that even where they have stumbled across such questions, they have warded them off with an instinctive feeling of danger. Realistic as well as idealistic explanations, scientific and philosophic alike, are not necessarily merely something added to a non-rational attitude to the world and life, any more than it would be possible or profitable in the long run to refuse to trouble about the disquieting inquiry of reason. May it not be the case that the rational emancipation (in which all science and philosophy are engaged) as such would be a tragical or, as judged by faith, a sinful necessity ? In that case, this movement which is indubitably for intellectual freedom would at the same time result in an untrue and wrong, and therefore disastrous, development, while on the other hand not to participate in this movement, in so far as such is at all possible, would not mean to avoid untruth, wrong, and disaster.

As a matter of fact this is the only answer possible from the standpoint of Christian faith. The whole effort of reason as such tends not merely to the emancipation of the intellect, but also to the intensification of a perversity inherent in the nature of actual man. It tends not merely to emancipation from a dull imprisonment in nature but also to emancipation from God. The opposition between idealism and rationalism is produced by, and receives a fixity that we cannot avoid from, the fact that when we proceed rationally we must look for either things in themselves or ideas in themselves instead of construing

F

both thing and idea as evidence of the reality of God as one personal spirit. This oneness is inaccessible to our thought. Hence it is not within the reach of any philosophy. For this oneness is a personal oneness, and can therefore only be made accessible by means of a concrete personal relation, i.e. by means of revelation and faith. Only on the ground of faith, i.e. on the ground of a personal revelation from God, can it be affirmed that God is the creator of the world, and accordingly that " the world " is actually to be thought of as " will and idea ", i.e. as the will and idea of God ; and that therewith the opposition between idealism and realism falls away. God is the true reality.

This statement, however, is not intended as a theoretical solution of the problem of knowledge : that would be to repeat the mistake of Thomist Aristotelianism. Theoretically the problem of knowledge remains as insoluble as before, and when a philosophy in the legitimate exercise of its power as thought avails itself of the thought of creation, this course always results in harm to both. Creation and God as creator are not theorems : they are no more philosophumena than they are mythologumena. A logical thinker will know that so long as he confines himself to thought he cannot speak of creation or Creator. Creation and a personal God serve to mark that thought has reached its limit. To come at them by way of thought involves the logician's *contradictio in adjecto* (contradiction in terms). For creation and personality indicate a breach in the continuity of thought. Creation is that fundamental stumbling-block for thought, the idea of *creatio ex nihilo* (creation from nothing) : the word " He spake, and it was done " dispenses entirely with cause or reason. Realism can never comprehend how reality can proceed from mind or will ; and idealism can never comprehend how there can be a " real " reality that is projected by mind from itself. The former recognizes only the principle of explanation, cause ; and the latter only the principle of comprehension, reason. We have no category that would serve to combine explanation and comprehension in a unity. Neither our idealistic nor our realistic thinkers can make the slightest use of " creation out of nothing ".

Creation then can be comprehended neither by idealist nor by realist thought. For the personal will of God or the word of God as the " principle " of all things, is neither cause nor reason, or rather both cause and reason. It is that coalescence of " real " and " ideal " for which we can give only an analogy, viz. human personality—with the reserve, however, that this *analogia entis* (Przywara) fails as an interpretation of the divine reality just at the crucial point : for men cannot create out of nothing. That the spirit, thought, and will of God form the sole self-existent reality and power, that the *decreta Dei* (divine decrees) are the sole " final causes ", and that the real world on the other hand, as a reality objective to mind, is the expression of divine " ideas "—all this belongs to the conception of creation as conceived by faith. No one ever reached it by intuitive thought, and any " thinking " it always involves at the same time the ceasing to think.[1] The mere logos apart

---

[1] For this reason idealism has always put the pantheistic or " panentheistic " conception of eternal coexistence or of emanation in the place of that of creation.

from the reality of the divine person is an abstract idea, the logos of philosophers, the mental ground, from which no way to reality can ever be found. If we think of God's creation without God, what we are left with is the mere datum, things as independent existences offering tough resistance : reality, or materiality as such ; but this is a mindless X which for this reason the mind cannot really grasp. The " thing " of the materialists, i.e. of extreme realists, is just as abstract as the idea of the idealists.

The creation (*creatura*) of which faith speaks is entirely different from the " world " which we know through ordinary or scientific experience. None the less creation (*creatio*) is related to this world. In the thought of creation as conceived by faith, i.e. as given only in the Scriptural revelation of Christ, the visible and existent world of our acquaintance is a hidden world, rendered unrecognizable, because severed from its union with its creator ; and thus the real creation is conceived as unknown and invisible. The known world is not a smaller but a greater problem to faith than it is to philosophy or science. For to faith it is not merely a theoretical but a personal problem concerning our whole being. Faith has to do with the " false " world that corresponds with the falsehood of sin. We do not know what a true creation would be like, any more than we know what a true man would be like. Knowing it in faith means knowing it only in the revealed word of promise, and hence without seeing it at all. It is the knowledge that it is wholly different from this world, and not to be known to us in its true condition until its reinstatement (cf. especially Luther's and Calvin's expositions of the *imago Dei* in original human nature, in their comments on Gen. i and iii).

The Bible, including the Old Testament, is not realistic in the same sense as modern realism, or any rational realism. It knows of no reality but a divine reality, i.e. a world which, to speak figuratively, is open at all points to the activity of a divine person, a world that God has " in His hand ". When Luther occasionally designates creatures as God's " puppets ", it may be allowed that he faithfully expresses thereby the thought of the Bible. It is wholly misleading to think we can appeal to the Biblical faith in creation in support of a monism, while of course admitting that the Bible conception of redemption is dualistic. In the Old Testament the world as created is indeed quite clearly separated from the existing reality by the Fall, and consequently the clearer the utterance given to the thought of redemption, the more audible grows the word about a " new heaven " and a " new earth ". The Bible knows nothing of the non-spiritual independence that modern realism gives to the sphere of material things and natural law.

It follows again that the Bible doctrine of creation also is quite different from that of Aristotle's metaphysic. Aristotle's doctrine knows nothing either of a personal God or of *creatio ex nihilo*. The God of Aristotle is the universal reason ; for him the " Creator " is not properly a creator, but a demiurge, a maker or fashioner of the world, and accordingly the relation of God to the world in this teaching is the prototype of all deistic systems. Nothing else is indeed possible, since Aristotle's whole metaphysic has a purely theoretical direction. It is the purest expression of the $\beta\text{ίος}\ \theta\epsilon\omega\rho\eta\tau\iota\kappa\text{ός}$, the type of all world-views—the very quality that makes it so genuinely Greek—an imposing æsthetic fabric. It is a fabric congenial to the contemplative type of thought, and just for that reason what is meant by creation in the Bible is not here at stake. For the latter is a stumbling-block to thought. Aristotle's doctrine of God and the world, being conceived throughout with a view to explanation of the world, starts exclusively from the side of the world. God is just a plausible hypothesis to explain that combination of matter and form which for Aristotle represents the most striking feature of the constitution of the world. There is not the slightest trace in Aristotle of the linking of man to the unconditional, all-controlling, sovereign personality of God, no trace of the thought that world and man alike are nothing apart from God. Hence it is unnatural to bring Christian faith into association with Aristotle—an association which by the very appearance of agreement between them constitutes a danger to our sense of truth.

Since faith possesses no theory of the world, and its understanding of the world is controlled by the concerns of man's personal history, it is not confronted with *two* problems, one theoretical, the other practical, viz. a problem of the world and a problem of man. On the contrary there is the one word of God which affords an answer to the question of knowledge and the personal question of one's conduct.

It is a well-known fact that realistic philosophy betrays its failure especially in the domain of ethics. The only realist ethic that is logically worked out is that of Epicureanism. Every other ethic—that is to say every ethic which is anything more than a doctrine of shrewdness, must borrow from idealism on the sly, either, as in Aristotle, by interchanging the empirical with the ideal concept of man, or, as in the fashion so prevalent to-day, by interchanging the instincts of sympathy with the altruistic sense of duty. This is immediately intelligible. For there is no ethic that is not a consciousness of duty, i.e. that does not involve a reference to a normative idea—not to a datum, but a mandatum. Hence it is out of ethics much rather than reflection on knowledge that philosophical idealism constantly grows.

A realistic ethic can be derived from either the Bios, or the Psyche, or culture. Thereby, it makes man a means to certain ends. The same is true of every ethic of impersonal " values ", of which we have recently heard so much. What gives attractiveness to Scheler's ethic and that of his school (Hartmann) is that it appears to offer *a priori* material values. This appearance arises from the fact that from the genuinely material values (which are not *a priori* but furnished by biology and psychology) a passage to the *a priori* is fabricated by help of the mediating conception of the values attaching to personality. The values of personality are in reality nothing but the concept of personality split up into its constitutive elements. Scheler's concept of personality, however, is richer and " more personal " than Kant's, but just to that extent it is less philosophical. Like Scheler's whole philosophy (of that date !) it is a mixture of knowledge derived from faith and from philosophy. The present day customary preference for the notion of value as compared with that of norm or law has its ground in the " biologism " and " æstheticism " of to-day. It should go without saying that a strict ethic of law, like Kant's, comes nearer to the Christian mode of thought than does any ethic of value weakened by æsthetic influences.

But even the strictest type of idealistic ethics, which has discovered the values of the self, freedom, and unconditional law, must, as we saw above, accept from realism the reminder that it is only dealing with the form of the good will, and that it never gets the length of prescribing conduct to a concrete individual. The inquiry after an ethic with specific content proves to be as vain as it is unavoidable. For a treatment of concrete situations which would avoid degrading man into a means to a mere thing, or a mere instrument of culture, and on the other hand, which would not merely serve the purpose of giving ideological absoluteness to a certain type of culture, could not take the form of any universal value, or abstract law of value, or any sort of gradation of " goods ". It would have to be at once absolute and concrete, it would have to be determined wholly with reference to the person and also the matter in hand, i.e. to be concentrated entirely upon the given moment in history and yet at the same time to have eternal validity. But ethics, or indeed any science that deals only in abstract principles, can know nothing of all this. The very thing that determines its scientific character, viz. the timeless and universal validity of the idea or norm, is opposed to any such concreteness. If a philosophical ethic diverges from strict adherence to universal law, it descends into a romantic type of individualism. On the other hand, the law which gives it its value can only legislate for man in general, and never for a given individual in a given situation, *hic et nunc*. Since the moral law, as we have seen, never gets beyond monologue, it remains related merely to the ego ; thus its ultimate and highest motive after all is self-regard. It never reaches a really concrete relation to a second party, a passage from the " I " to the " you ". In the end, everything indeed depends on its principle of self-regard, of legislation for oneself, taking one's stand on oneself ; autonomy is its fundamental principle. But this very principle obscures what is peculiarly true of man—that he is a sinner : that at bottom the self is not good, but is a will in contradiction with divine goodness. Sin is not merely contradiction of our own law. If we take that view of evil, we are not taking evil seriously. We flatter ourselves that evil does not ultimately affect or lay hold upon us at all. Seriously understood, sin is contradiction of the

divine will, so that the innermost self and the good
have really fallen into isolation from, and opposition
to, each other : it is severance from the ground of
existence and therefore not merely a matter of a man's
mental attitude, but of his personal existence. The
ego has its basis in the fact that God addresses us.
As personal, the word of God is the ground of the
reality, as well as of the knowledge, of the self. Outside
this ground there is neither a real ego nor yet any
knowledge of the ego. It follows that sin, which is an
(attempt at) severance from the ground of existence,
is also the original falsity—emancipation from God.
It has its ultimate ground in the will to be independent,
that is to say, an unconditional, as opposed to a con-
ditional, will to be independent. The opposite of sin
is thus not virtue—that is a notion that belongs wholly
to the rational doctrine of emancipation—but faith.
The core of sin is unbelief, the small-minded and at the
same time arrogant assumption that even with God
a man must have regard to his rights (for all these
points, cf. the story of the Fall). Only thus do we
reach a personal understanding of evil, viz. as with-
drawal from an originally existent personal relation.
It is not our attitude to an abstract law that makes
us good or evil, but our attitude to God. The question
is whether we are willing to have life by gift of God,
or of our own motion. The Fall is a declension from
the Creator and Giver of all good, a false independence
and self-assertion, i.e. such as is directed not against
the creature but the Creator, a self-exaltation. It is
a will that wants to be more than it can, and over-
reaches itself by this self-exaltation. In short, it is
a freedom that, through over-estimating itself, becomes

slavery, since there can be no such thing as freedom apart from God. It follows—and here comes in the (so to speak) metaphysical element in evil—that sin is at the same time lack of freedom for good, the so-called original sin. " Whoever sins is the slave of sin."

Once man has turned from God, he no longer has the divine unity of life in prospect, but a divided self consisting of an unspiritual concreteness and an abstract spirituality, i.e. the sensuous element by itself, and the law or idea by itself. The divine thought and will are now mirrored for him in the idea, though only in perverted form. The law, the idea, is God, so far as He can still be known by man after he has become perverted. The idea is accordingly ἀνάμνησις, a recollection of his original condition, now lost, but *not* a recollection of the personal God. The idea is a " broken light of God ", an isolated ray of truth. God as idea is not the living God. In the idea, the fundamental relation of God and man appears precisely reversed : instead of being the first, God becomes the second ; in place of an original certainty, He becomes the object of man's search ; from being the One who gives the good life, He has become the One who demands it of us ; and so in place of ability in and through God, comes ability of oneself independently of God. The point in which sin and God's reaction against it in the law come in contact is autonomy when viewed from man's side, but guilt when viewed from God's. This is implied in the twofold sense of the German word " Schuld " : the fact that we are familiar with the good as duty (Schuldigkeit) is in itself an omen of perversion, guilt (Schuld). Thus at this point the emancipated ethic of

reason comes into collision with faith most sharply.
Idealism says, " If I know that I ought, then I know
that I have worth, and can." Faith says : " If I know
that I ought, then I know that I am separated from
my origin, and therefore cannot." The fact that we
ought to do the good, that it appears to us as mere
matter of obligation, and hence foreign to us, is the
decisive expression of our separation from the divine
good. The knowledge of good and evil arises only
after the Fall. " Neither Christ nor the devil has a
conscience."

It is obvious that it would not do to evade the above-mentioned
difficulty (*vide supra*, p. 69), and the conclusion we have just
drawn, by opposing " autonomy " only to " false heteronomy "
and equating it completely with theonomy. Theonomy is a
novelty in contrast to both autonomy and heteronomy, just as
faith rises above the opposition between realism and idealism.
We must not take autonomy away from the *autos-nomos*. It
is just the problem for faith to discover a possibility of escaping
the " false heteronomy " without succumbing to a false autonomy, and it is solved in a way that can no more be called
" autonomous " than the living God of revelation can be
equated with the Platonic idea.

The emancipation of reason, as most clearly expressed
in the principle of autonomy, is thus, as Hamann
puts it, really a " misunderstanding between reason
and itself " ; it is perception's (Vernunft) refusal to
perceive (vernehmen). But it is an error of the
Romantics to think that there is another and better
human solution than that of the autonomy of reason,
of obedience to a self-contained law of reason. Of
course, Romanticism will always have historical
justification as a basis of protest against " the abstract
law ", against the " universal mentality ", but it will

never be capable of stating and supplying what it really intends. In so far as it thinks to supply this, it will conduct us to a still more dangerous ideology than that of rationalism or idealism. For it lacks the capacity for the sober reflection on itself that reason possesses in criticism. A return to his original state is barred to man as he actually exists in history. The sin of separation from his origin is not merely an act, but, as far as the act takes place at all, it is at the same time destiny—and this is the core of the doctrine of original sin. Granted that the law as an independent power " came in between " by way of a provisional expedient,[1] yet now it is a fact and it impresses its stamp on man's life in history to such an extent that law may be equated with humanity. But along with the law of reason, and therefore with life in history and with humanity, unfreedom also is a fact. The consciousness of responsibility is constantly accompanied by the consciousness of guilt, and this is indeed the unavoidable, (as even Kant puts it) the " inborn " guilt, the *peccatum originale*, the *a priori* of all history. Law and sin together are the characteristics of this interim-stage of reality, of which the third mark is death.

The standpoint from which we make this affirmation must be manifest. We make it from the same " place " as that from which we are in a position to assert the reality of sin and of a personal Creator-God : in other

[1] The law as an independent power is not the same as its substance, i.e. the eternal will of God. In its unity with the revelation of God's grace it is called " the covenant " in the Bible and in Christian doctrine. This latter conception excludes " legality " as clearly as obligation, but the divine claim on our obedience is included as an element in faith.

words, from the revelation of Christ in the Scriptures. The believer can see autonomy, law, and sin in this close relation because he has seen through the sinful nature of the legal relation itself, or rather because it is made known to him as sin by the revelation of the real God as One who freely gives goodness, life, and His very self. If the real God is the God that gives freely, and if the true man is the man endowed by Him with life, then man's independence and autonomy become the original falsehood ; yet in fact that extreme of falsehood which comes very near the extreme of truth. For it is only before God that a man can really and, if the term be permitted, absolutely, lie, just as it is only before God that he can be true. It follows that the " place " where the moral crisis took place is the historical situation in which the thought of the moral law and of a legal relation to God was most strenuously realized, i.e. in the Pharisaic development of Judaism. It follows that the message of God's revelation, which is His act of reconciliation, betokens at the same time a conflict with legality, in other words, justification for sinners by grace alone.

This term (*sola gratia*), speaking as it does of exclusive divine action, seems far removed from the sphere of the ethical problem. Yet Christian faith recognizes in this term the new foundation for action which lies beyond the opposition of realism and idealism, of duty and fact, and by which we can arrive at a really concrete ethos. Concrete ethical action is only possible where the real God definitely claims the real man.

Concrete ethical conduct will mean living in a faith which is obedience, and in an obedience which is at the same time faith. " The just shall live by his faith," i.e. live as an object of benefaction, of grace, as one who stands before God in the contingency and sinfulness of his concrete existence, and whom God subjects again to this " contingency "—and by this very act releases him from its contingent character. To see world, man, and life as they are seen by God, i.e. as " justified " in the midst and in spite of their sinful contingency and belonging to God even as they are, is the mark of the new ethic, the ethos of love. But since this love, in distinction from all else that bears that name, is not a principle but an ever constantly renewed dependence on the divine gift of grace, it follows that the new ethic can equally well be spoken of as a doing away with every ethic. For in essence this love is no more an obligation than it is wedded to a specific result, although in virtue of being both an inner disposition and a power to perform it takes all other conduct under its control.

At this point, however, it is specially needful to call to mind that faith is not a possession that man has at his command, but actually an utterance and gift of God, which of himself man can never bring about or in any way command. Being still man, i.e. a visible phenomenon in history, the believer does not cease to be a sinner and therefore still " under the law ". This holds good with regard to knowledge as well as conduct. Both these problems faith can only regard as solved in the sphere of divine promise. " We live by faith and not by sight." Thus we remain in the world, where knowledge is needed, where the opposition of idealism and realism is insuperable, where the moral life has to be ruled by law, where there will also constantly be rebellion against any rule of law, and where such rebellion will never be simply wrong (Romanticism). Yet by means of faith this life of ours comes under a different point of view : its provisional character is recognized, the law is no longer an ultimate principle, the legal attitude is done away, and we can see through the misunderstanding between reason and itself, although it is not thereby set aside. Hence there cannot be a Christian science, state, or culture, but only a co-operation of the Christian believer with state, culture, and science ; this co-operation will not find its principle in these latter, and hence it will be only an indirect co-operation, clearly conscious of the provisional character of all man's historical life.

Moreover, just for the same reason there can be no knowledge of God but the paradoxical knowledge given in faith. The contradiction that clings to our whole existence finds expression in the fact that the divine reality also can reach us only fragmentarily, as a light broken by false reality, and is only visible to us in this fragmentary way. In this fragmentariness lies the contradiction, the stumbling-block to reason. But here again we must needs draw a distinction. Revelation is only a stumbling-block to that reason which proclaims itself as a final court of appeal even before God. Hence the stumbling-block is not so much to reason itself, as to the arrogance of reason, our self-sufficiency in virtue of reason. But the arrogance of reason is not a fault of some particular men : the reason which is ours as men is as such always in the grip of this vain conceit of autonomy. It follows that the gulf in knowledge exists in all of us, and that it cannot be closed. There is no escape left for us whereby we could form a unity out of the antitheses between sense and reason, realism and idealism, reason and revelation. Revelation is incomprehensible even to the believer himself, he too is constantly confronted with the possibility of a stumbling-block. The solution of the puzzle which is in the " possession " of faith does not amount to " insight " : our vision is not right through, but in a " dark mirror " : the assertions of faith are one and all paradoxes. The " natural " man takes offence at them, for they are mysteries in which God reveals Himself as the Incomprehensible. They never become " illuminating ", but all through life remain merely credible, and certain only to faith. We never attain to the tranquillity afforded by sight : that is reserved for eternity. Thus faith itself is not the solution, but faith knows of a future solution which by the grace of God shines beforehand into the present. Faith is distinguished from everything else, e.g. from mystical experience, precisely by knowing of the solution, the redemption, without as yet possessing it. This knowledge of the future event constitutes the present possession and the joy of faith. It is knowledge of that event to which revelation points, when partial knowledge will be terminated, and when opposition between reality and truth, between abstract idea and concrete character will cease ; and faith can take away the final poignancy of this opposition even now.

The creation of the world and man is one of the great subject-matters of theology. It is because the world is a mirror of the divine Spirit that it can be known at all. Otherwise it would be a dark chaos of which we could know nothing. God can be discerned in this work as spirit and power. Were this the sole truth, man would perhaps behold God's face in nature as in a mirror. But in fact this is only one side of the truth. The world is also a veiling of God, a cracked mirror, a mixture of sense and nonsense, and man has run away from home and lives on the husks that swine eat. Reason which was created to be a mirror of God is spoilt and split. The *analogia entis* cannot attain a real knowledge of God (*cognitio salutaris*).

He who thinks he can know God from this world is deceived either as to the true grounds of his faith, or has perhaps a knowledge of that world-*Nous* that Aristotle calls God, but only an uncertain, vague knowledge even of this.

It is not merely that faith and revelation present riddles to reason : nay, the greatest riddle of all is rational man himself, with his insuperable vacillation between knowing and not knowing, likeness and hostility to God, between scepticism and mysticism ; man, who precisely in his rationalism is the most irrational, indeed anti-rational, of all beings. History affords a thousand instances of what faith declares, viz. that apart from faith, man is incapable of seeing himself as he is. He cannot coordinate the truth of cynicism and enthusiasm but swings from one to the other. Worse than all, he makes for himself an equation which causes this oscillation to appear normal. Having these two aspects, he manifests, at one and the same time, the Creator's glory and its perversion. And owing to the perversion he cannot himself be aware of it : for he can only know it at the point and in the degree in which the original truth is restored to him.

The whole man, as so described, with his openness to challenge and with a certain, though never clear, consciousness of the fact, is the " point of attachment " for revelation. The " capacity " which manifestly suffices the divine Creator as a point of attachment is no special sense, but our consciousness of ourselves as human, and this again is only the inner division as it is reflected in consciousness. But there is of course in the " natural " man one point in which this consciousness of division is clearest, and which is at the same time the centre of his life in history—I mean the religious consciousness.

Chapter 6

THE ELEMENT OF TRUTH IN SUBJECTIVISM : REVELATION AND RELIGIOUS EXPERIENCE

There are two radical forms of subjectivism which are diametrically opposed to each other in purpose, but actually have often enough overlapped, viz. radical scepticism (e.g. the Sophists) and radical mysticism (e.g. India). When watered down by the rationalism of cultivated life and society, scepticism becomes a philosophy of the senses and mysticism a romantic individualism. When the maxim, so characteristic of the Sophists, that " man is the measure of all things ", was taken in all seriousness, it entirely destroyed the concept of truth, and thus also destroyed itself. But although it has been a thousand times refuted by this argument, scepticism constantly survives in virtue of the fact that you cannot give it any definite bound. As a principle, its relativism can easily be refuted—since every principle, including the relativist, is put forward as " true ". But in face of all particular propositions which are asserted as true, no fixed limit can ever be set to scepticism, for even " pure reason " is never pure but, in so far as it is we who propound it, is also relative because human. Knowledge has no absolutely valid contents—not even the forms of thought, in so far as it is we who know about them.

Neither can mysticism be fully refuted ; and hence

it is always cropping up again. It derives its power from the consciousness of identity that underlies every proposition thought to be true, in other words underlies our whole mental life (cf. Augustine's argument about *veritas*). Mental life is only possible at all on the presupposition that we " participate in the logos ". But mysticism rightly maintains that this point of identity is presupposed by every definition, and hence can never itself become a definite thought, but is the source of every definite proposition. Hence the point of identity is itself only real in the form of an un-mediated unity, i.e. of a feeling ; thus the point of identity is the feeling in which the Ego and the All are identical. But irrefutable as mysticism is, as long as it consists merely in making this reference, no less does it entangle itself in contradiction as soon as it makes of this origin, not indeed a definite system of thought—that would amount to speculation—but a definite experience, occupying time ; only in this way is mysticism a form of life.

Neither scepticism nor mysticism can ever remain true to themselves. The only thorough-going scepti-cism would be the complete self-suspense (ἐποχή), that ventures on neither action nor thought of any kind. But this would be to bring life to a complete standstill, and so would be impossible. The only logical mysticism—to which the radical mysticism of India makes a near approach—would be a complete submergence in the All, without the slightest interest in the dichotomized life of seeming reality, or in culture and society. Both schools betray a profound disbelief in themselves by their participation in man's life in history and the struggle for truth. You can be neither a thorough-going mystic nor sceptic, because a logically consistent course of life would be the opposite alike of mysticism and scepticism. Consistency means logical sequence, conformity to law ; and law is the opposite of both scepticism and mysticism. Thus while both have an element of truth, neither is really practicable in life.

Scepticism could only be overcome, without loss of its element of truth, if there were presupposed an absolute communication of truth which excluded man as agent. It would be a truth that retained the sentence that " all men are liars "—i.e. that no human assertion as such merits the predicate of " true "—without thereby involving itself in self-contradiction. Such an elimination of man, however, could not be accomplished by starting from human consciousness, but only in the form of a communication of truth, of divine *revelation*, whereby God should posit Himself as the sole truth. Similarly a mysticism which retained its element of truth could be superseded only by a union with the divine Absolute in virtue of a datum which itself belonged to the historical world and hence permanently tied us to its historical life, i.e. an absence of mediation on the basis of the most perfect mediation. That, however, is what is meant by revelation in the Christian sense : but be it understood that no mere idea of revelation has this emancipating power. For neither one nor the other, as an idea of ours, would reach this truth. Only real, historical revelation, a revelation in which that judgment and this union actually take place, and which can only be conceived because it has taken place, could provide the emancipation. In Christian faith the denial of any human power acquires a decisiveness which is not merely critical nor, again, merely sceptical, because it is not merely theoretic but matter of fact, viz. doubt. Moreover in it unity with God acquires a depth that is more than unity of disposition or even mystical self-abandonment ; it is that " mystical " state which the ancients called *insertio in Christum*. Personal unity in life with the Redeemer is the essence of the redemption to which faith looks forward.

We have not space to enter upon the many modified forms of sophistic subjectivism which are so much in vogue to-day. These hybrid forms are all sensationalist, fictionalist, or pragmatist philosophies. What brings them under the head of rationalism is their starting from a " reality " known rationally to some science, e.g. a science of psychology or biology. The result is that all of them without exception have as their presupposition the world as envisaged by natural *science*, no matter how anti-rationalist may be their demeanour in other respects.

Their subjectivism accordingly presents a positively comic contrast to the confidence with which these philosophers champion—and demonstrate—their theory as " correct ", i.e. universally valid ! A transition to Romanticism, i.e. to a quasi-mystical conception of the world, is furnished by the systems which combine intuitionism with this pragmatism, as, e.g. does Bergson. It is interesting to observe how Bergson becomes the complete speculative idealist when he speaks of intuition. In this case Neoplatonism steps into the place of pragmatism. We have thus no occasion to enter into any special discussion of this group.

But philosophers of religion are not interested in scepticism as such, nor yet mysticism, at least in its most radical forms, since both make a philosophy of religion impossible, the one abolishing the religion, the other the philosophy. What interests them is rather that modified form of mysticism that admits of being included in a rational system of culture and science, i.e. mysticism as " religious experience ", and this quasi-mystical religious experience regarded as the principle of religion. By the Enlightenment, religion was reduced to certain moral or metaphysical commonplaces, and this was justly brought into discredit by Schleiermacher. Since then philosophy of religion has held chiefly to the alternative solution offered by him. Here the " essence of religion " was found in this very " religious experience ". When given a normal formulation by the philosopher of religion this is a sort of mystical feeling of unity on the part of the subject with the All, or the divine side of things, but of such a kind as not to shatter the rational fabric of science and culture. It is thus an irrational side or " province " within the general sphere of reason. This mode of conception has a decisive feature in common with that of the Enlightenment—and of idealism (*vide supra*, p. 37)—viz. that religion is something capable of a general definition, in other words that there is such a thing as the " essence of religion ". It is only distinguished from them by removing this " essence " more decidedly from the objective life of reason. None the less it is only by being subsumed under the higher concept of reason that a philosophy of religion becomes possible from this standpoint.

But precisely by so doing, the philosophy of religion, while bent upon understanding the nature of actual religion, adopts a position that contradicts every actual religion. If all the religions of the world have a common element, it consists in being based not upon a universal, but on a concrete feature, viz. on acts of revelation. Of course, the philosophy of religion declares this concrete feature to be, not the primary basis of the religion in question, but only the occasion that serves to liberate the religion. It is not the essential, but only the accidental and individual element of the religion in question that has its roots in that concrete feature. But such an assertion amounts to nothing less than that the feature in which philosophy of religion sees the essential element is fundamentally different from that in which the religions themselves see it. The revelation in which the religions believe is self-deception, whereas the religions know nothing of the kind of revelation in which this philosophy of religion believes. To the actual religions the essential element is the reality, the experiential presence of real gods, i.e. the contingent entrance in time of something that is not contained in the spirit of man himself nor in the objective environment of his life.

While the religious philosophy of Schleiermacher and Hegel clearly brings out this opposition, more recent systems, like those of Otto or Scholz, give the impression that they are really concerned with the conception of the aforesaid concrete revelation (cf., e.g. the beginning of Otto's *The Idea of the Holy*, p. 11, where prominence is given to the reality of the fact of revelation, with a primary reference to the realism of W. James). But in the crucial interpretation of the phenomenon of religion the author speedily falls back on the immanent categories of critical (*a priori*) or of speculative idealism (the innermost core of the ego), so that we find in Otto such formulations as " Religion has its roots in the impulses and depths of the rational spirit itself " (*Vishnu Narayana*, p. 153). There is *one* disposition and *one* " shaping impulse—which everywhere begins the process of giving form to the life of religious idea and feeling " ; and one disposition " which produces similar effects in different domains because it has a uniform character " (ibid., p. 150). With such a conception it is impossible to reconcile what the religions, and also what the Christian faith style revelation.

In order to decide whether philosophy of religion is right or not in its interpretation of " revelation ", in spite of its contradiction of the actual religions, we must ask whether it is really possible to exhibit the " essence of religion " alleged by the philosophy of religion as the common basis of all religions, or, speaking more guardedly, as at least the meaning of those religions—i.e. the thing they primarily intend. A careful scrutiny of the actual structure of religious consciousness goes to show that this is not the case. We will begin by taking as our thesis the conclusion of our discussion—that there is no such thing as a common " essence of religion ".

On the contrary, what is disclosed to us by the historical facts is a great variety of religious phenomena fundamentally differing in structure. On the one hand are those religions of which we can only speak in the plural, because each of them is what it is through its relation to a concrete datum consisting in revealed facts, in which something " other than the world " seems to be proclaimed to man by active self-manifestation. Such are the religions in which gods are the object of belief and worship. This gives religion a thoroughly objective character and definite content. Such religion has reference to non-human divine personalities that are self-existent and have more or less individual characteristics. In that case the mark of personality is inseparable from divinity. Indeed, the entire interest is centred there. The existence of gods is the primary datum of such religions. Not to acknowledge, or to deny, the existence of these self-existent personalities is the extreme of godlessness, while conversely to acknowledge them as real and powerful is the essence of the piety which the cultus expresses. It is not in the first place the cultus that makes the religion ; on the contrary acknowledgment of the reality of the gods is the religious presupposition of everything belonging to the cultus. This theoretic and practical assumption of the fact that the gods exist finds expression in the cultus and makes the latter the central phenomenon of religion. It follows that the cultus itself has objective character and is a real transaction. It gives expression to the reverence for the gods ; it is an attempt to establish between those two realities, gods and men, a relation that will be favourable to men and honourable to the gods. Accordingly it takes the form of contribution and counter-contribution, of a real exchange. That is why religion, in this case, becomes a mediation between two spheres of will and power, and this mediation is itself a means and not an end. What men want is not religion, but something by means of religion. And what God bestows is not religion, but something for the sake of religion. There is here therefore a real conflict, and the aim of religion or the cultus is to set it aside. The most important elements in cultus are : (a) prayer that invokes the name of God, i.e. acknowledges His personal existence and power ; and (b) sacrifice that attracts or restores His favour (expiation). This type of religion we propose to designate " objective religion ".

Opposed to it and completely diverse in nature is

the " subjective " religion of mysticism. It is subjective not only in the object to which it refers, but in the mode of this reference. The object of faith is not the gods, i.e. persons who will definite things ; rather in this case there is found a universal divine sphere of a neutral character. Religion has the neuter-form of the Holy, the Divine. Correspondingly, piety is not reverence for the will of Another, but on the contrary a drawing of this divine It to oneself, or a self-transportation into the divine region. Thus it is not a relation of idea and will with reality which is their object, but a relation of identification with one's ego, tending to subjectivity, i.e. it is a feeling. The aim in such religion is not recognition of difference (reverence) but fusion (love) : a relation in which we are not face to face with the object, but within it. Even in this case there may be remains of religious action (dances, swinging of bull-roarers, intoxication, ascetic exercises) ; but they have no longer an objective, but only a subjective orientation ; their aim is not to make any offering to God, but to transpose the ego into a certain condition, viz. that of the closest possible identification with the neuter divine reality. Such religion is thus not a matter of mediation, but an end in itself. What it wants is itself, not some objective thing, for in such religious states one possesses what is itself divine. It follows that this divine thing cannot be a person. For personality implies a limit to my existence and a limitation of the range of my power. What is sought in this case, on the contrary, is the annihilation of personal limits, viz. a state which cannot be mediated.

These two types of religion are so different that

they would be quite unable to recognize each other as manifestations of religion. The very thing which is of supreme importance to one is, in the judgment of the other, the thing to get rid of. One lays the stress on using mediating action for venerating the divine Person in His independence, and on an ulterior purpose. The other stresses the collapse of all personal limits and immediate enjoyment of religious experience as an end in itself. Objective religion will disparage the mystic as an atheist, while subjective religion will disparage an exponent of the former as a worldly man. They cannot regard each other as examples of religion. It makes no essential difference to the opposition whether in the case of objective religions we think of people who are merely " church goers " or of those that are moral, and whether in the case of the other type, we think of mysticism that is essentially natural and orgiastic, or mysticism that is refined and spiritualized. In moral religion the personal limit is accentuated by the consciousness of guilt, and in higher forms of mysticism the immediacy is further raised into consciousness of absolute identity. But there can be no bridging of the opposition that is more than apparent, i.e. by modifying or confusing the opposed forms. A real bridge between the two could only be provided by an event that could no longer bear the name of religion, i.e. a personal self-communication on the part of God, which would be neither a mystical experience nor an act of worship nor a moral performance on the part of men ; neither a removal of personal limits nor a human expiation, but a divine expiation in the form of a divine self-communication. But of this religion can know nothing ;

because in it, religion—in both senses—would be done away.

It is of the essence of Christian revelation that in it the limit, the interval between God and man, is disclosed in unheard of fashion by the revelation of the divine wrath against man's sin. Yet at the same time this interval is done away by the revelation of God's mercy to the sinner who in spite of his sin is declared by a divine utterance to be made one with God, by a reconciling mediatorial act of God Himself. We can perhaps show how the meaning and purpose of subjective and objective religion, though in mutual opposition, are declared in a paradoxically incomprehensible way by the Christian faith in revelation : but of course we cannot show theoretically whether that declaration is true, nor what it signifies not merely for abstract thought, but also for the whole life of the individual.

If there is no such thing as a common " essence of religion ", how comes it that we can none the less classify these two phenomena under the common notion of " religion " ? It is no accident that the problem of the " essence of religion " first arose on Christian soil. For only if we start from Christian faith, which stands above the opposition of subjective and objective religion and can no longer be subsumed under the idea of " religion ", as will presently be shown—only so is it possible to bring these two disparate phenomena together. But even now this can only be done when we see that the unity resides not in them but in something else, while a relation of mutual exclusiveness exists between them. We may understand the opposition between mystical and objective religion as a schism, as a lapse from truth. We cannot do this, however, on our own resources, by means of a general idea of religion, whether speculative or empirical. We can do it only from a standpoint that is not our own, but that of the revelation of God in Jesus Christ. Subjective and objective religion alike are " partial truths " which cannot be brought together because they are also deformed truths.

Speaking now from the standpoint of Christian faith as the only point from which we can gain understanding, we say that the deformation in objective religion consists in setting up a false reciprocal relationship, viz. a partnership between God and man which finds expression primarily in action that is not directed to God Himself, but to some end dependent on Him. This deformation is not confined (say) to religion in the form of cultus ; it is found equally or even more in moral religion. Hence Christian faith is not concerned with the distinction between a religion of cult and one of morals.[1] To say that moral performance is meritorious and that man's salvation depends on human works involves as great a perversion of truth as dependence on performance of the cultus, and indeed is an untruth the more dangerous in proportion as it approximates to the truth.

The deformation in the case of subjective religion consists in failure to see the real boundaries between God and man, between the sinful creature and the holy Creator. Mysticism overleaps both by its doctrine

[1] In this connection we may recall the *Epistle to the Hebrews*, in which Christ appears precisely as the fulfilment of a religion of cult.

of immediacy. In this point it resembles speculative idealism, which is indeed its correlate in the realm of thought. The guilt of sin, taken seriously, means an irreparable overthrow of immediacy such as could only be restored by a divine intervention, an act of divine mediation. Thus in the case of both subjective and objective religion, the deformation is man's attempt at using his own resources to make good what is lacking in his life, whether by asserting a claim on the gods or by transplanting himself into the divine sphere. In either case we have to do with a failure to take seriously the actual and vital trouble, the real cleavage between God and man. This cleavage is only acknowledged when we confess that the " integration " cannot come about except through a divine act, a real setting aside of an obstacle recognized as real, and effected by God Himself doing what man ought to do. And this can only become a matter of knowledge when such an act of God Himself actually takes place —a mere idea could only amount to a solution from man's side—and when, conversely, right knowledge of the actual situation as between man and God is attained only by way of that divine event. Only thus does faith in God's justification of the sinner come about. Justification is foreign to all mysticism, because it seeks not to experience grace, not to believe in it, or, to say the same thing in other words, because it knows nothing of a Mediator. But with faith in justification even religion comes to an end, because man knows that even his piety, his religiosity, everything which as a devout man he actually is, does, or has, all come under the judgment of God. He no longer expects salvation from them—as the mystic does from his experiences of grace, or the " religious " man from his good disposition. Rather he expects it from God in spite of them. This is the crucial point of all religion.

At the same time, it is its fulfilment. For this is the solution for which every religion cries aloud, viz. actual divine help. The presence in religion of this consciousness of a need that only God Himself can supply constitutes the immense significance of religion for human life, despite all deforming of that consciousness. Religion in the sense of longing for God is the greatest of all man's characteristics. But religion in the sense of silencing that longing is flight from God, a sham solution, an evasion of God's serious demand and our own surrender. Hence religion is always also defiance of God. The supreme religion has brought this to crucial expression. The revealer of God's righteousness is also the victim of that religious defiance. Here, if anywhere, the divided " essence of religion " becomes manifest ; it is only in this crucial point that its meaning becomes known.

It is when man realizes himself in his distance from God, when he becomes truly conscious of his " *humanitas* " as a forfeited nearness to God, when he realizes that his best, even his religion, cannot help him, but only brings him into danger—it is then that the other factor that truly saves comes back into view. And conversely, the true knowledge of himself can only arise when the factor that really saves becomes perceptible to him. It follows, however, that it takes place in man's " inmost heart " as an entirely *inward* experience. Even a Christian can say that subjectivity is truth (Kierkegaard), but he knows that it is a subjectivity that is no longer his own. It is an event that is a matter neither of moral disposition nor of mystical union, but that nevertheless works out in a fresh moral disposition and in a consciousness of union with God ; it is the inward utterance of the external word of God, i.e. the Holy Spirit. The doctrine of the Holy Spirit is the Christian answer to the truth in subjectivism, the doctrine of that inwardness which is not in the least degree our own.

CHAPTER 7

THE ELEMENT OF TRUTH IN HISTORICISM : REVELATION AND THE HISTORY OF RELIGION

The fact that our century, perhaps beyond any other, pays such attention to history may be explained in saying that modern times are characterized by an emancipation largely indebted to history. From a psychological point of view, historicism might be accounted for primarily by reaction against abstractions, against the rationalism devoid of history and the individualism of previous centuries. Historicism arises naturally or instinctively where history does not itself constitute a problem, and this because the men concerned live entirely in the line of history, i.e. in the tradition of the past and in attachment to society. Such historicism is only conscious of itself to some extent when it comes into conflict with rationalistic individualism. Of this type of historicism we shall not speak here. There is another form of historicism which is not in the first place of a traditional character but in which the element of tradition is valued only in connection with a kind of historicism that is a matter not in the least of instinct, but of fully conscious thought, viz. the absolutist historicism of the Roman church. Its principle is not tradition or history, but the Christian revelation. It is primarily a form of the

Christian faith. Between Catholicism and Protestantism there exists at the outset a fundamental unity and a common opposition. They are fundamentally united in confessing a unique revelation of God in Jesus Christ, and also in opposing any belief in revelation that springs merely from idealism or mysticism or from religion in general. Only inside the ground common to both does the opposition between the two confessions come to light, and the essence of this opposition is historicism, or the principle of tradition.

Side by side with Scripture, the standard which it shares with Protestantism, the Roman church puts another tradition, i.e. a continuous revelation side by side with that which is unique. The Church is *realiter* this historical entity. But since she or ultimately the Pope is the sole exponent of Scripture, she takes rank above the primary standard of revelation. The authority that finally decides is actually that of the continuous history : the principle of history has triumphed over that of revelation. This is another kind of historicism with which we cannot concern ourselves further at the present juncture.

What we are rather concerned with is the historicism in which historical development has become the crucial fact in all interpretation of the world and life : I mean the relativist historicism of the present day. This historicism is not an outcome of history as such, but only of a particular conception of history. This conception of history can be briefly characterized by naming as its parents the individualism of the romantic school and the naturalistic doctrine of evolution. It is from romanticism that modern historicism derives its mode of regarding every living phenomenon as an individual event. Not merely separate men, but also peoples, cultures, periods, and regions, marked by a similar culture, are individualities having an inner organic unity and regular characteristics of their own, and these at the same time give them their creative nature. With this romantic idea is combined the Heraclitean as modified by the modern conception of causation. It teaches that whatever exists, including whatever lives, is held in a process of ceaseless change, which itself is explicable by causation and perhaps has a certain tendency (" evolution ") inherent in it.

Sometimes yet a third thought is combined with these, but this is really opposed to the predilections of historicism : it is the idealistic conception of growth as the self-unfolding of the idea, in other words, Hegel's philosophy of history. But such a conception can only be worked out in connection with, or rather as the outcome of, the philosophy of absolute idealism. The reason is that history can only be interpreted as the unfolding of the absolute spirit when you start from this spirit as already known. The conception is therefore fundamentally irreconcileable with a relativist type of historicism : accordingly we shall wholly disregard this line of thought.

Both individualism and evolutionism lead to the same issue, viz. the relativistic type of scepticism. If everything is in a state of flux and if nothing transcends individual existence, how are we ever to reach any absolute affirmations of universal validity ? This scepticism of course shares the fate of scepticism in general : it must brook having its attention called to the contradiction that is inherent in it. If all is in a state of flux, if nothing that emerges in the course of history has an absolute validity, this must also hold good of the corresponding conception of history : a consideration that involves its collapse. Moreover, you cannot in fact teach this scepticism, without rendering yourself ridiculous, since teaching presupposes validity and also a truth that transcends the individual and is independent of time. If everything is in a state of flux, the fact of flux itself can no longer be established. That there is a problem of history can only be seen at all from a point above history.

But the problem of a relativist historicism cannot be disposed of merely by such general considerations as to the unserviceableness of relativism as a principle. For the " historist " [1] will constantly meet all abstract considerations with the phenomenal evidence of historical reality, which always presents itself in individual and changing forms. Accordingly we for our part cannot avoid raising the question as to the nature of history. This investigation will lead to the discovery, surprising to many people, that behind that simple phrase " historical fact " lie very difficult problems. If we start from the work of the historian, to whom we look in the first place for instruction upon facts of history, we perceive that the prime task he sets himself is the reconstruction of the complete " film " and the complete " gramophone record " of the past. (We need not here take notice of the fact that even this task cannot be performed without constant reference to the " spheres of value ".) But no historian would rest content with such a

---

[1] It goes without saying that the historist, i.e. the representative of the principle of historicism, has nothing to do with the historian as such, although historicism is perhaps to be met with in special frequency among historians.

reconstruction of the apparent facts. His further intention is to give, so to speak, a physiognomical interpretation of these phenomena. He inquires into the " why " of them. And in this case the " why " has a twofold significance : there is the " why " of explanation, i.e. that which inquires into cause, and the " why " of understanding, i.e. that which inquires into meaning. If all the sciences from astronomy and geography to religious sociology should make their contribution to the *explanation* of such a historical phenomenon, as (say) Plato, this would still do nothing towards the *understanding* of it. What is explained causally is still not understood : and conversely, what is understood can never be explained. We understand what we can put into relation not with " cause " but with " meaning ". What, e.g. is " meant " or signified by the ideas of Plato we understand only when we disregard all causal occasions—in fact only when we disregard the individual Plato, just as we have to disregard all personal and psychological factors in order to follow a lecture given by a mathematician. The disregarding of causes and persons is a condition of the understanding of truth.

As soon as this is recognized, our view of history will include an element that lies outside the circle alike of what is individual and what is changeable. In so far as we understand history at all, we stand outside the stream, in a relation to it that is above history and outside of time. But we have not yet come in contact with what is truly historical. What serves to explain to us the complex idea " Plato " (causes, such as race, nation, period, etc.) is something in the nature of a universal, a complex of causes, and

therefore *not* Plato. What makes Plato intelligible
to us is a universal, a complex of meaning, a set of
ideas independent of the individual, and so again not
Plato. But what then is Plato, and what his talk and
doings, that we can speak of them as his ? The
answer of romanticism is : That is the secret of
individuality. But we only need to point out that all
life, all existence indeed, is individual—that between
the individual existence of a tree or bird and that of
Plato there is a difference not of quality but only of
degree. This fact alone shows that the conception of
individuality does not bring us directly into contact
with what is truly historical. Individuality is a conception belonging to the realm of nature : it is fundamentally the quality of being a datum. It may be
difficult or even impossible to strip this datum fully
bare, but none the less it is fundamentally nature
discoverable and awaiting discovery.

Leibnitz's conception of individuality is, however, essentially
different from and deeper than that of the Romantics, e.g.
Schleiermacher's. For Schleiermacher the proposition holds
good *principium individuationis est materia* (matter is the
principle that gives individuality), and he constantly repeats
the assertion that, even in the case of spirit, individuality arises
only through the universal spirit's entering on material existence
and, so to speak, breaking itself up therein. For Leibnitz on
the contrary individuality is founded in a creative act of God
and therefore, so far from excluding eternity, actually includes
it. But this conception of individuality is metaphysical ; it is
not one that starts from the fact of God addressing man and
man's self-determination in reply. Hence in this case again
individuality, even while spiritual, is still a datum, spirit-nature.
Accordingly it too can only be known—so far as it is capable
of being known—by means of the universal, i.e. as a concrete

example of the universal, although it differs from the individuality of romanticism by being a concrete example of an eternal metaphysical constant. As far as it can be understood, instead of remaining beyond all understanding as a mystery that is as it is, it has to be construed from the universality of the idea, as a specific instance of it, and not a " transaction " or self-determination. Thus even Leibnitz shares the view that history is a palpable mass of spiritual existence, albeit of an existence extended in time. Here again that essential characteristic of history is lacking—deed, decision, the ego as a being that determines itself in response to the divine " thou ", by whose summons it was called into being. Hence for Leibnitz also man is conceived essentially not as man, but only as a concrete example of the universal. And from our discussion (p. 83) we know why : it is because his conception of man is metaphysical and not of the character yielded by faith.

Plato is far from being merely an individual. As an individuality he is only quantitatively defined. He is thus the great genius that included in himself more elements of truth, beauty, spiritual power, etc., than other men of antiquity ; he is in the first instance a wholly unique combination of what all other men also are, but in quite unique proportions. But this is not to define him as man at all, i.e. as a historical person. Plato is more than an individual, he is a man, a personality, he has self-determination. The true subject of history is not merely what is individual, but what is personal. And this is not, as is individuality, a datum, even a datum difficult to conceive, but fundamentally what is not a datum. Personal decision is not, like individuality, a mysterious combination of elements of being, but is fundamentally different from everything that we can conceive of as a universal : it is the Creator's call and man's decisive response. Individuality is *made* by the Creator ; it is an *object*.

Personality is addressed as " thou " by the creator. Man is *called* into existence. And it follows that his life in its specifically human and truly historical quality is lived by way of a *definitive answer* to this call.[1] Above all individuality stand responsibility and the freedom that has its basis there, a freedom which makes every moment of life a crucial moment.

But this, the true nature of history, is not now grasped by any " historian ". The historian may indeed look for its true nature in that direction. As a good physiognomist he will not interpret the phenomena of history as individual data, but as *facta*, *res gestae*, deeds. According as " history " approaches or keeps aloof from this standpoint, it is regarded as " profound " or " superficial ". But history in the proper sense is outside the circle of even the most profound " history ".

What the " historian " sees is never the historical element proper, the vital decision, but only the after-history or consequence that more or less approximates to decision. To use a parable, he sees the tree that is struck by lightning, and perhaps crashing to pieces in consequence of the stroke of lightning, but never the stroke of lightning itself. He sees the clouds of smoke and the stream of lava, but not the crater in eruption. What we call history is only the outside, no more than a surface reproduction, which still needs interpretation even where the historian combines the genius of a Shakespeare with the knowledge of a Ranke. For the act of decision is at bottom a secret which no one betrays because no one knows it—not even the autobiographer !

[1] See my *Die Mystik und das Wort*, p. 94 f.

The reason is that we are an enigma to ourselves when we make our decisions. We know that the decisions that make up our personal life are not the final reality of our personal life. We know—even as critical philosophers, like Kant, we could have some knowledge of this—that life, conceived in terms of act, does not consist of pieces but is a unity. Our moral personality, full of contradictions as it is, is yet a unity in act. Every one of its decisions proceeds from a deeper, fundamental decision. Without ceasing to be decisions, they are yet consequences of a single decision which cannot be included in a relation of temporal succession or be conceived as their *prius* in time, and yet it is their *prius*, their basis. As the thousands of notes in a musical score serve to express but a single musical thought, so all our individual decisions are at the same time the expression of an original decision which carries or begets them all *qua* decisions ; and just because this original decision cannot be comprised in any temporal scheme, it lies beyond the reach of any psychological perception, including even self-perception.

The decision which is the deepest reality of our being is at the same time its profoundest untruth. We are all of us wearing a mask. We know it is so, but we no longer know rightly what there is behind the mask. History, in the sense recognized by us, is a masquerade in which each plays his own part. There is no one who crosses the stage without the mask— not even the noblest, and least of all the author of confessions ! There is none who can take off his mask. It belongs to the very nature of that original decision— in which we have all become alike and through which we have all become so pitifully unlike—that once it has been made, it can no longer be seen. For it is a lie and it creates darkness, while at the same time it assumes the character of destiny, i.e. makes it necessary henceforth that all decisions should be in correspondence with it. Decision is that which has reality only as a response to that divinely gracious call to us, and in which therefore our highest worth as created beings finds expression : and yet it is at the same time the factor on which depends the loss of this divine nearness and worth : in other words, it is sin. Our divorce from the source of life is at the same time a divorce from freedom and truth—a mask that cannot be laid aside again because it is our " *persona* ".

It is only from this standpoint of the "Urgeschichte" or primordial history that the general character of history can be known at all. " Urgeschichte " is the germ of all history ; what the historian relates to us as " history " is its manifestation in space and time.

There is no unambiguous word for what is here intended. But when we designate it " Urgeschichte " and thereby conjure up the possibility of confusion with primitive history in the chronological sense, we believe we have sufficient justification for so doing, alike on philological and on intrinsic grounds. In a similar sense Goethe spoke of the " Urpflanze " or primordial plant, and meant thereby something which, while it was real, could not be classified in an evolutionary series of temporal causes. The origin of species does not really belong to the empirical sphere : it is an " Urgeschehen " or primordial event : indeed it would seem that even exact science is obliged to have recourse to a phenomenon that falls outside the world of causation in space and time, i.e. to " Ur-tatsachen " or primordial facts as the ultimate data of all physical processes.

We can, however, only speak of primordial history when we are concerned with personal decision, and this means, with a response to the divine call. Of other primordial facts, "Urtatsachen," we can speak metaphysically as we can speak of an object : but we can only speak of "Urgeschichte" as participants, i.e. as persons who have themselves been spoken to. In other words we can only speak on the ground of faith. It follows that primordial history cannot be a matter of historical and psychological perception but only of faith.

History is a middle term between what has meaning and what has not, between the transient and the eternal. Nature has no history : to speak of natural history is a misuse of the term. History belongs to the domain of humanity : only what is human can have a history. But humanity is at once made in God's image and yet marred, knowing but ignorant, fleeing from God while yet longing after Him. All human culture, whether in the deepest or the most superficial sense, has this double aspect : it is at once flight from and longing after the eternal. It follows that a conception of history that is both cynical and realistic, e.g. materialism, is just as true and also just as false as a conception which is both ideological and idealistic. The former sees in history a mere causal procession, i.e. "chance", while the latter sees nothing but teleology, i.e. pure meaning. The truth is that history consists of fragments of meaning—the word fragment being here translateable literally, as "broken piece". History is only to be understood as a break-away from actual meaning. It is only thus that we can obtain access to its central problems, and above all to the problem that goes deeper than all others, and that is the essential problem of history, viz. the relation of the individual to society. It is through the connection of the individual with the race—and at the same time the separation of the individual from the race—that history comes to be.

It is the specific characteristic of the being *humanus* that the very quality that makes the individual a member of his kind (*humanitas*) at the same time separates him and makes him an end to himself. Participation in *humanitas* means participation in the condition in which he is not merely a member of a species, but a person. History reveals to us a mutual seeking and fleeing on the part of the separate individuals and the community and this is explicable neither by biological causes nor ideal aims. All history is an attempt at an integration (redintegration) of what has become disintegrated, and at the same time a progressive disintegration (think, e.g. of the emancipation of reason). To historical man, it appears impossible to determine his relations rightly without a false breaking loose from, and a false association with, the community. Thus history consists chiefly in a constant building up and pulling down of forms of society such as always betoken at once life and death. But all this is " foreground ", " after-history ", and not " Urgeschichte " or primordial history. We have no longer any knowledge of the right, i.e. the original relation between individual and society. In the state in which we now confront one another, individuality and collectivity are already deformed and therefore can never be coordinated again without doing violence to one or the other. That primordial decision which is the real *a priori* of all history, that truly disastrous " Urgeschichte " which cut us adrift from the ground of life, was also the destruction of primordial society, a cutting adrift from the ground of society, its dissolution into separate figures each with a false independence. Individual existence, in the sense now known to us, also belongs to the masquerade of history. Our own age for fully a century has revered personality as the " supreme blessing of the children of earth ", and may be said at length to have gained a certain understanding of this masquerade.

There is therefore no such thing as a unity of history, and no possibility of understanding it by means of such unity, i.e. there is no possible philosophy of history. Philosophy consists in interpretation on the basis of unity, of a universal, of some principle. The notion of a history of the world as a unity is a bastard begotten of Christian faith and rationalism. Christian faith knows nothing of any history of the world in the sense of a unity. Its unity is not historical, but that which belongs at once to " Urgeschichte " or primordial history, and " Endgeschichte " or the consummation of history, i.e. history not as moved by forces within itself, but within its relation to a creative and redeeming God. This is a relation that cannot be fitted into the frame of profane history. It is not the course of history as such that is of interest, not the fact that it is controlled by an immanent system of law, whether causal or teleological. Rather what is of interest is the lightning-flash in history of what lies behind history, the effective self-assertion of a factor that by its very nature does away with history, viz. the reality of divine revelation. It is this third, " middle " point of the Urgeschichte, the revelation of God in Christ, this event, open not to observation but to belief, between Creation and the Fall on the one hand and a redemption out of history on the other—it is this through which it becomes possible for us to speak of " Urgeschichte " at all. The Christian believer sees history as an intermediate realm, a mixture of indefinable character. It is lit up, however, as by lightning by the history which is both primordial and ultimate and which blazes up at its central point. There, i.e. in Christ, the meaning and the absurdity of history, its created unity and its ruin by sin, its attraction to God and its distance from God, its beginning and its end, are visible outside history.

It follows that the history of religion, which is also the inmost current of history, can be understood solely from the same standpoint. The reason why the history of religion is the inner shrine of history, why religions are the soul of all culture, is that in religion there dawns upon us something of the meaning and yet the absurdity of life as a whole and of historical existence. In religion we are most clearly conscious of the rift in existence, the open wound, the suffering and wrong of the present. In it we realize somewhat of the fact that in regard to God we are sick men, and that healing is to be found in God alone. Religion as consciousness of God is the place in man's nature that lies nearest to his original union with God, but also to the point where he " broke with " God. In its history, therefore, religion is the human element which stands in the nearest relation with revelation.

In Söderblom we have a representative of modern historical thought. He maintains that for us the history of religion in general has taken the place of natural theology. We believe for our part that the relation between reason and revelation, which constitutes the problem of the old natural theology, will still be the central problem of theology after the problem of the history of religion and revelation has long ceased to be a burning question for us. The reason is that this latter problem does not really affect existence, but raises a purely theoretic issue—except perhaps in the conflict between Christian faith and mysticism. Nevertheless Söderblom may be so far right that at the present moment the problem of the history of religion stands in the foreground of discussion. The novelty in this mode of posing the question depends mainly on the fact that only recently has Christian faith come into closer contact with the highest forms of eastern religion. Theologians of earlier times had to discuss their position with regard only to the comparatively inferior religious systems of classical antiquity and also to the various forms of the religious philosophy of late antiquity which, while intellectually lofty, had little religious power. Moreover, we have been made familiar with such an abundance of facts of religion by the modern science of religion that we cannot avoid the idea of a more or less complete continuity of stages of religious development. This idea suggests the possibility, on the one hand, of ensuring the highest rank to Christianity, but on the other, of inserting it wholly in the context of universal history. Since the time of Herder, Hegel, and Schleiermacher this scheme of a universal spiritual evolution, including also " the Christian religion ", has become a sort of scientific axiom which anyone who claims to be scientific must simply accept. This thesis of idealism has been rendered unobjectionable to theology by the circumstance that the conception of the individuality of religions seemed to give due and proper place to the peculiar character of Christian faith.

The modern relativist theory of gradation, according to which the Christian religion is merely a phase, though perhaps the climax, of the general history of religion, is irreconcilable with the Christian belief in revelation. Equally irreconcilable is that entire interpretation given by philosophy of religion, which deals with revelation and supplies the basis of the theory. By revelation the Christian believer means something fundamentally different from an individually unique expression of the universal essence of religion. The romantic conception of individuality, which Schleiermacher was the first to identify with that of revelation, stands to revelation in a relation, not of likeness nor even of kinship, but of opposition. Christian faith is inseparable from the confession, scarcely tolerable though it be to the educated man of to-day, that the Christian revelation stands related to all religion, not as an individual to other individuals of the same species, but as another genus. It is the relation of the truth of God to man's search for truth, or as the answer is related to a question. It follows that Christian faith, or the theological standpoint as distinguished from that of the philosophy of religion, makes an immediate assertion. The assertion is that when we have regard to the quality of the Christian revelation, instead of its being a phenomenon coming under the observation of secular history, we find it stands just as much outside the history of religion as outside the sphere of reason. In making this assertion it may be taken altogether for granted that here again the word " outside " signifies a double relation only to be taken in a dialectic sense. We cannot affirm of Christian revelation what faith affirms, without at the same time making this distinction, just as the earliest testimony of Christians added to the confession of Christ the further declaration : in none other is there salvation (*vide supra*, p. 48). That confession and, therefore, this distinction are based on faith alone. To demand a scientific basis for it would be as foolish as to demand a scientific proof for the revelation itself.

That Jesus was something besides founder of a great religion, like Buddha, Zarathustra, or Mohammed, is no more capable of scientific demonstration than that he was the Son of God. If it could be proved, it would be the proof of something quite different from what faith means.

What we can and should demand from scientific investigation, however, is a demonstration that the structure, the inner meaning, and the coherence of the historical phenomena of religion, differ from the Christian faith about revelation in such a way that even on scientific grounds the assertion about continuity is shown to be an arbitrary construction, and not to correspond with the facts. We may perhaps further expect that Christian theology will at least attempt to interpret these historical phenomena of religion : such an attempt, it is true, could not be unhesitatingly recognized by the scientist on account of his special presuppositions, but at least it could not be rejected on scientific grounds but only on grounds derived from his general view of the universe.

In essaying this interpretation, we may make a certain use of the ancient doctrine of the *logos spermaticos*. But it is particularly needful to make a clear and fundamental distinction between the sense in which we shall do this, and the use which was made of this conception in the period of the Enlightenment, and by idealism. We begin by making the revelation in Christ our starting-point in every respect. Only as we start from him, the incarnate word, can we discern the " partial truths " of the various religions and the " partial meaning " of the historical developments of religion, just as the various parts of a pyramid can only

be surveyed from its summit. Our first thesis would
be that Christ is the fulfilment of every religion. But
taken by itself it would be false : it must straightway
be supplemented by a second thesis—that Christ is
also the judgment upon every religion together with
its history. Measured by him the truth as well as the
falsehood of all religion becomes discernible as nowhere else. There is no such thing as a steady approximation to him : for all approximation signifies at the
same time a growing distance. The evidence of this is
furnished actually by the history of religion, even when
the comparison with Christianity is made merely from
the mental standpoint of phenomenology. The history
of religion shows not only a development in the direction of " Christian religion ", but a no less decided
development away from it, and this too at the culminating points of that history. The " law of parallels "
which has recently been advanced proves on closer
examination to be just as much a groundless hypothesis
as the notion of the " essence of religion ". Nowhere
is the opposition to Christian faith, though accompanied
by an unmistakable approximation, so pronounced as
it is at the acknowledged culminating points of the
general history of religion. The apostle's question :
" Is then Christ divided ? " must in fact be answered
in the affirmative as far as the history of religion is
concerned. It is indeed precisely the " meaning and
yet the absurdity " of the history of religion that in it
Christ is so divided that the parts can never be put
together into a whole.

Let us now go back to what was adduced in the
preceding chapter : save that this time we take a
section not across, but down the length of, the history

of religion. When once our attention has been turned
to the irreducible opposition between " objective "
and " subjective ", the whole history of religion takes
the appearance of a tree with two trunks which,
springing from a common root in the historical
beginnings of religion, diverge a little above the
ground and get further and further apart in proportion
as they grow taller. The question as to the historical
origin of religion is no longer the central point of
interest now that the naturalistic theory of the Positivists
has passed its vogue. As regards the inquiry into the
" essence of religion ", clearly we cannot expect to
learn much from the primitive beginnings of religion.
On the other hand this very question, contrary to what
we might expect, again commands a higher degree of
interest when we start from Christian faith, because,
in a way, Christian faith comes nearer to the primitive
religions than it does to any of the more " highly
developed " religions. In this case also what is childlike comes nearest to divine truth, though it be only
as a parable of that truth. On the primitive level all
those elements are still side by side, which diverge in
their later development. They must diverge—so says
optimistic idealism ; must, and yet never ought to
diverge—so says Christian faith. In primitive religious
consciousness there is as yet no distinction of rational
and irrational, nor of religion, ethics, law, culture,
and nature. It is the fact that man is " still " a unity
that makes the charm of the primitive. Owing to
this unity, however childlike and below the plane of
intellect, what is primitive serves perhaps as the best
parable of what is " primordial ". At the same time
it has ultimate validity, as it cannot be recovered in

any process of historical evolution or by any logic immanent in history. In all religion then there dwells a " numinous reality ", a terrible earnestness for reality, which is increasingly attenuated in the course of higher development.

Nowhere can we see this more clearly than in the development of ideas of God. To the extent that they gain in the quality of personal spirit as they evolve out of the impersonality that attaches to nature, they lose at the same time in " numinous reality ". Again, to the extent that the gods are raised out of their material limitations—the most significant symbol of which is their transference to the sky—they also become more distant and less real. The classical example of this change is the pantheon of Homer, where the " spiritualizing " clearly means a forfeiting of real living power, of " awfulness " in the religious sense. Hence the impulse to mythologize can now seize upon them and draw them down increasingly from the level of a religion that involves the whole man to that of æsthetic fantasy. The same decline is seen also in the sphere of cultus, which loses its non-rational and positive character. The gods become protectors of the civil order, and their worship becomes a part of civil life. The content of the cultus, embodying the divine will to be obeyed by men, is approximated to civil utility. It loses that character of strangeness in which pre-eminently the divine will had formerly found expression as the " wholly other " ; rather it is humanized and is increasingly identified with the laws of the common life of society. Evidently the goal of this development is the point that is reached in the religion of the Enlightenment, viz. where the will of

God coincides with the laws of nature and of morality. Sin is no longer an outrage on what belongs to God, but an offence against civil regulations. The thought of the "wrath of God" gives the impression of ascribing a human passion to God : the deity is deprived of any will of His own. He becomes the world-law and there is scarcely any distinction now between a religious man and a good citizen. The feeling, so powerful in primitive religion, that divine life is something strange, incomprehensible, and dangerous, gives place to a unification of divine and secular ordinances. Thus in this case spiritualization comes to mean rationalization in the sense of conformity with the laws of nature and reason. This involves at the same time a buttressing of historical conditions as they are. And that means that spiritualization becomes a matter of increasing remoteness from the revealed reality of a divinely " other " and strange world, together with a transition to the consciousness of reason as immanent in the world.

It is accordingly intelligible that the type of investigation that aims at knowing not rationalized but " really religious " religion has preferred to turn its attention to the other branch, that of mysticism, as the domain of the irrational. In the case of mysticism the drift seems to be in just the opposite direction. The more pronounced the mysticism the clearer becomes the consciousness of opposition to what is of " the world ". The holy is just what is not-world, not-man, not-culture, not-reason, and indeed not-something. Thus it comes into sharp opposition to the world of phenomena and all definite forms of existence. The distinction of this " Theopanism " from " Pantheism " is superficially reasonable.   It serves to express the true meaning of mysticism, so far as the latter will permit itself to be expressed in thought.

R. Otto lays special emphasis on the distinction between pantheism and theopanism.   When, however, he asserts that between the two there is the greatest conceivable opposition, he is partly right and partly wrong.   Thus, for example, he calls Spinoza a decided theopanist, and Bruno an equally decided pantheist, and yet everybody knows how much Bruno's idea meant to Spinoza.   Just the same statement holds good regarding India.   In the Bhagavadgita, " theopanist " ideas pass imperceptibly into pantheistic ;   we have only to recall that well-known passage ;   " I am the taste in the waters, the light in the sun and moon . . . the pleasant scent of the earth . . . the life in all beings," etc.   Nor is it surprising. On both views the main statement is the same, it is only the emphasis that is different :   God is the All.   Whence it also follows :   All (that exists) is " at bottom " God.

What corresponds to this theoretic position in the practical sphere is recoil from the world, indifference to the life of culture as exhibited in history.   The deity is the Only One, in whom all specific realities fade away.   In the same way to be religious means to enjoy that mystical experience, that feeling of absorption in the All, which, because it alone is an end in itself, makes one indifferent to all other forms of life. Mysticism includes the " dying to the world " characteristic of the hermit, the ascetic, and the saint. The sublimation of the rude forms of nature-mysticism, marked by all sorts of intoxicating experiences, into the lofty mysticism of the spirit is brought about on the one hand by freeing the idea of divinity from all that is accidental and individual, and by elaborating that increasingly abstract idea of deity which is only accessible to the man of speculative gifts. Hence intellectual mysticism is always highly aristocratic, a quality it shares with philosophical speculation which is akin to it and into which on its intellectual side it tends increasingly to pass. But even the " experience " becomes (so to speak) more abstract, independent of accidental stimulants or ecstatic excitement. It passes over into tranquil meditation, absorption in the conception or the intuition of the One. The goal of pure mysticism is the acosmistic sort of intuition and life characteristic of India, with a technique that aims at putting off the world and complete severance from the social life that makes history. But the mysticisms of Neoplatonism, of Persia and Arabia, and even of medieval Christianity—though this is constantly held back from developing naturally by the dogma and life of the church—all show fundamentally the same features. Mysticism has no power of building up social communities and therefore it can never play a part in history except as a creeper on the trunk of an objective religion. It is the religion of a small minority who earn the veneration of others as saints by their life of renunciation, unless they become suspect on account of their " atheism " or indifference to objective religion. They remain merely on the fringe of the history of religion ; it is only by joining in monasteries—which itself involves a certain compromise with the world—that they attain to a more considerable influence in history. But even where their circle of influence is further increased by the formation of a third class of half-monks, the ideal is still that of abandoning the world and bare toleration of it where relation with it is unavoidable. The opposition of this development to that of objective religion is thus clear. In the latter we have spiritualization in the form of rationalization, with a tendency to confuse the sacred sphere with that of secular culture, whereas in the former all the elements of rational culture are absorbed into the exclusive feeling of being the Only One. In rationalism is the tendency to law and historical organization, in mysticism the tendency to the infinite and unlimited ; in rationalism, the secularization of religion, in mysticism, the whole of life swallowed up by religion ;   in rationalism, religion attached to the culture and state, in mysticism, the hermit life of the saint and the cloister.

But this opposition in the directions of development only becomes fully manifest when we bring particularly into the comparison those higher forms of religion in history in which the tendency to extremes seems to be held in check, and which, therefore, claim special attention from those who are in search of instances of a " law of parallels " with Christianity. Of such forms we need take serious account only of the " theistic mysticism " of India and the prophetic religion of Zarathustra. Eastern Buddhism (Amida Buddha) and perhaps the Hellenist religions of late antiquity would only be relevant in a much less degree. We must confine ourselves to the first-named two.[1]

[1] The account here given is founded, apart from the well-known works on Hinduism, solely on texts accessible in translations (in English in the collection *Sacred Books* : in German in the collection edited by R. Otto, and also the translations of the Bhagavadgita by Deussen and Garbe). Yet, in view of the interest that controls R. Otto's solution in particular, we can hardly expect that, as far as our problem

In point of fact the air that breathes in the Bhakti literature of Hinduism is different from that in the Upanishads. It must often have happened that a reader of the Bhagavadgita, which is the most important book of religion in this class, has experienced something of the awesome astonishment with which Wilhelm von Humboldt first entered upon this new world. We may leave on one side the question whether a popular monotheism coming from North-East India, of which otherwise we have only indirect knowledge, lies at the base of this real summit in the history of religion, as has recently been conjectured. This theory contributes but little to the understanding of the bhakti type of religion. For this is another case where there can be no question of a definite and victorious monotheism that taught equally the independence of the divine personality and the reality of the world as a creation of His. This religion, while formally theistic, constantly overturns into a system of thought in regard to which we should find difficulty in saying whether we ought to call it theopanism, nature-pantheism, or polytheism. The reality of the numerous popular gods is not contested, nor is their worship deprecated. There is no attack upon polytheism, such as took place in Persia and Israel. Even the savant who proposed the " law of parallels ", and who appeals particularly to bhakti mysticism in support of it, finds himself compelled to admit that " everywhere theopanism peeps out through its theism ". Nay, the one among these theists who is furthest removed from the universal theopanism of India " holds firmly to the belief that the world is the body of Isvara and asserts a kind of unity between the soul and the deity " . . . " And they all remain mystics " (Otto).

Often in a surprisingly " Christian " form, this Indian " theism " stands for the doctrine of the nearness and the love of God, of the grace that alone saves, of the kinship of the soul with God, and so on. But we find in it nothing of such central themes of the Bible as the paradoxical unity of

is concerned, a knowledge of all the original literature would necessitate any different judgment. Even the works of Grierson and Glasenapp yield a similar picture.

these conceptions with their opposite, the judgment, wrath, and unapproachableness of God, or his " zeal " for His " honour " which He will not relinquish to another ; or His absolute difference from all creatures ; or His will to reinstate the fallen creation by judgment and new creation ; or an act of atonement and revelation on the part of the Mediator, who conducts God's business on earth as a divine and yet real man, as *agnus dei qui tollit peccata mundi* (the lamb of God that taketh away the sin of the world) ; or of a final divine goal for the world of nature and history. As a consequence, it is not God's forgiving and redeeming activity that occupies the central place, but the religious experiences of the saint. We may grant that these experiences are ascribed to grace, but they are never thought of as those of a sinner saved by grace, a culprit acquitted who yet remains permanently under both judgment and grace. Rather they are those of an advancing saint, who by means of infused grace actually becomes so holy that in the end he necessarily becomes partaker of the Eternal. (At this point Amida-Buddhism approximates considerably to the Christian belief in justification. But in other respects the points of opposition are more profound. Still less can there be any question in the eastern form of Buddhism of God the creator and establisher of His dominion.) India knows nothing of the problem of guilt in the Christian sense. As a consequence it also knows nothing of reconciliation, which comes to man as word, as speech from God, and has to be simply believed by man, and which has its basis in an actual event just as really as guilt has. We might say that India is in conflict with " Pelagius " but not with " Osiander " ; with a sinful worldliness, but not with a sinful holiness.

We might carry a good deal further our list of contrasting parallels : e.g. India is familiar with incarnations, but plurality is an essential feature of them, whereas in Christian faith it is just the uniqueness that is the decisive feature. All religion in India aims at the holy man as the embodiment of what religion means, while in the Bible there are no holy men. The man of God as an individual retires wholly into the background. The greatest of all the prophets is anonymous, and we have not the slightest personal information about him ; hence we refer to him by means of an emergency-name as " Deutero-Isaiah ". The prophet as such does not desire to be anything, to have any ability or possession but a word of God which he proclaims aloud to all the world and in the delivery of which his life is consumed. The tolerance of Indian religion strikes the modern man agreeably in comparison with the intolerance of the Christian religion. It is tolerant because it is mysticism, and knows nothing of a controlling divine will and a divine history. All mysticism is tolerant because it is purely subjective. It has no place for such an utterance as " The zeal of Thine house hath eaten me up ". The God of mysticism has no jealousy, because He is not a will. There is no conflict in this case, because there is no goal.

We may conclude by quoting the words of a distinguished scholar : " The attempt altogether breaks down to see in Indian theism and bhakti-religion a manifestation related to Christianity. The Indian bhakta takes his stand on the ground of his inherited view of life. The world is at once real and yet, as a manifestation of the One, it is an illusion ; the numerous gods exist, and at the same time are mere appearances of the One. Behind even the idol his vision penetrates to the universal power, and the fundamental element in bhakti is heart-felt love that craves a personal object of love, but then transcends limits and can lose itself in what lacks all positive quality and personality." (Sten Konow in Chantepie de la Saussaye's Manual, 1925.) Of course, where even Christian faith is confused with mystical experience, where the concrete case of meeting with God, or the unique revelation of God in Jesus Christ, or the $\epsilon\phi$' $\mathring{a}\pi a\xi$ of apostolic preaching is conceived merely as a particular and accidental special form of the universal religious impulse, it becomes possible to represent even Indian mysticism and Christian faith as overflowing into one another. Once Christian faith has been transformed into mysticism, no great skill is required to establish a " law of parallels ", since as a matter of fact mysticism has everywhere developed if not in exactly the same, yet mainly in similar ways.

It seems to me then that we should consider much more seriously the possibility of establishing a parallel between the religion of Zarathustra [1] and that of the Bible, particularly of the Old Testament. We might easily imagine the Zarathustra of the Gathas in the company of, say, the prophet Elijah. There is here no doubt about the personality and singleness of God, or of His position as sovereign ruler over the world— a world, too, which is real. Ahura Mazda is Lord and King of the world and men. He is holy will. Hence it is his will to be the object of personal reverence, and so he reveals himself personally through his prophet (in this case we must confine ourselves to the singular) by his word, which is the sacred rule of life. The religion of the Gathas is ethical religion, and accordingly has reference to a people : it has a historical purpose.

---

[1] Despite the fact that some philologists despair of reaching an unobjectionable interpretation of the earliest Avestan literature, we may and we must venture an attempt to give a separate presentation of the religion of Zarathustra. " Le sens général des Gatha est connu et il y a maintenant accord entre les savants qui les étudient " (A. Meillet, *Trois Conférences sur les Gatha de l'Avesta*, 1925). Our presentation is founded primarily on the translation of Bartholomae. The quotations from Geldner and Lehmann come from their articles in *R.G.G.* and *Chantepie de la Saussaye.*

There is a conflict in process between God and evil, but the final victory of God is certain. Hence there is also a warfare against " lying " polytheism and its priests, and a prospect of a final judgment of God, carried out on moral and religious principles. There is an eschatology—features, these, which are wholly wanting in the picture of Indian religion. This religion consists in faith and obedience : there is no trace of mysticism. It recognizes personal prayer, but not meditation. I venture the opinion that there is no point in the whole history of religion where a comparison with Biblical faith thrusts itself on us so much as here. A blood-relationship is also shown by its capacity for being assimilated as seen in history (cf. the stock of Persian ideas in Christian eschatology).

But could it be chance that the religion of Zarathustra remained a mere episode in the history of the world, or that only a short time after the death of this great man a compromise was concluded with polytheism and intricate ritual, which buried the noble religion of Zarathustra beneath a mass of religious rubbish ? Zarathustra has vanished from the world without leaving behind him a heritage of his own. Yet this consideration must not take the place of an examination of the religion. Zarathustra's religion is ethical religion. We might say, more exactly, legal religion. " In the Avesta, religion is called law, and the Persians had no words to distinguish the conception of religion and law " (Lehmann). Its power and greatness depend upon this strict, moral legality. The opposition which this man of God saw more clearly than anyone else in the history of religion as an opposition of the good and holy God to the corruption that is in the world, is so comprehensive that he divides mankind also into good and evil. On the one side stand the good who are friends of God just because they are good, on the other stand the wicked who are enemies of God. But the Gathas show no trace of the thought that the opposition passes through the individual man, that " in Thy sight no flesh living shall be justified ", that no man is worthy to fight in the army of light. The good survive the judgment because they have been good. The central point of the Bible message—the grace of a righteous God, His nearness to those who are of a broken heart, His faithfulness to the unfaithful—is wholly unknown to this religion. " Zarathustra has no knowledge of the conceptions of remission or forgiveness of sins " (Geldner). " Nothing is said of grace or clemency " (Lehmann). The moral law or the law of life coincides with the will of God. God does not stand freely above His law, He is not the mysterious living God of the Bible, who is wroth and forgives, who is now distant and now near, who is inexorably stern, and who yet condescends in mercy to the weak and the fallen. We shall seek vainly in the Gathas for any hint that God could reveal Himself by the death, indeed the death on the cross, of the righteous one, that God's truth presents a crisis to the morally good just as much as to the morally evil, and that there can be godlessness in the good as well as in the evil. Man's deepest distress, the guilt of the man who would fain belong to God, is unknown. God stands not above but under His own law. " In virtue of this knowledge, Mazda decided for purity and life, whereas the devil preferred death and impurity. It is this choice which so to speak made him the

true God and gave him his power " (Lehmann). Since
God is thus identified with His law, there can be no
forgiveness. No line can be drawn from such ideas
to Jesus Christ the crucified. The idea of vicarious
suffering would necessarily shatter this religion of
rigid legality, and therefore unlike the prophetism of
Israel it is not " a foretelling of Christ ".

This renders superfluous the inquiry as to how far,
say, the moral theism of late antiquity might be
reckoned a parallel to Christian faith. The faith of an
Epictetus in God is much further removed from that
of the Bible than is Zarathustra's. It is simply a
religion of the type characteristic of the Enlightenment,
i.e. an ethical rationalism interpreted in a religious
sense. At a still greater distance from the faith of the
Bible stand the syncretic forms of Hellenistic religion
which constitute the historical environment of primitive Christianity and furnished it with a considerable
part of its vocabulary and perhaps other elements too.
We shall have to discuss the question of causal connections in the next chapter : just now we are concerned
only with a question in phenomenology, viz. as to
inner kinship and similarity of structure. Anyone
who has once grasped the significance of concrete
revelation, of uniqueness, for Christian faith will not
be tempted again to bring it into relation with the
mythologies of Hither Asia or Egypt (e.g. the myth
of a divine Saviour who dies and rises again). In these
latter it is precisely the constant repetition of this
" pseudo-event " which is the characteristic feature
—to say nothing of the radically different conceptions
of sin and reconciliation.

When exposed to the light and at least as applied

to Christian faith, the law of parallels dissolves into mere illusion ; and with it vanishes the idea that there is one continuous development in the history of religion. This appearance can only be confused with reality so long as religion in general, and even the Christian faith in particular, is identified with mysticism. The reason for this is that despite all its variety of shades mysticism is in fact always and everywhere essentially the same thing, because it is detached, and consciously detaches itself, from concrete history.

A peculiarly contradictory relation is thus disclosed between the history of religion and the general history of the spiritual life. Religion has her part in this : she herself is " spiritualized " by the development of the spirit. But she does not become " more religious " thereby. The spiritualization takes place in one of two directions : either law in place of caprice and unity instead of manifoldness, or infinity in place of finitude and the unlimited instead of the limited. In the first case it leads by way of personalism to the universal reason of the world, in the other to acosmical and theopanist mysticism. But in both cases the specific mark of religion, consciousness of real revelation, of concrete divine self-manifestation, fades away. In both cases the result is something timeless and therefore unreal.

Of course, religion has played its part and, throughout history, worked its way into man's spiritual life in general ; nevertheless this life is characterized by an increasing emancipation of culture from religion. The character of reality originally attaching to the revelations claimed by the religions cannot keep its place in face of awakening reason. A rational culture

K

can only enter into association with weakened forms of religion, with that of the Enlightenment on the one hand, or with a mysticism that has either been rationalized or adapted to culture on the other : for neither the massive personalism of religions that acknowledge gods nor the absolute, non-historical subjectivism of thorough-going mysticism can satisfy the claims of a life of culture in the widest sense.

Persons deliberately in pursuit of culture have no use for any religion that is not entirely " spiritualized ". It is therefore a shrewd observation on the part of Positivism that history shows an increasing decline of religion.

None the less all reason and all culture arise from religion, and without it are bound to become sterile. Without it, fully freed from it, they dwindle into mere civilization with an *art pour l'art* and a *science pour la science*. New foci of culture have never yet originated except in connection with strong uprisings of religion. Culture by itself has no power of self-renewal. It would have to draw renewal from religion—and yet cannot do this. For the type of spiritualized religion that has accommodated itself to culture has not the power. On the other hand the man of culture can no longer accord trust to a living and powerful type of religion. He discerns in it too much of the merely numinous and too little of the logos ; too much " accidental reality " and too little rational necessity or truth. The renewal of man's spiritual life could not come from religion and the products of its history without being at length compelled to lose itself in mere civilization and finally in weariness of life. The renewal can only come from the region where the eternal logos, the truth itself, is revealed as reality. This, however, would not be in any way the history of religion or of the spiritual life, but the revelation of their origin and end.

The history of religion is, as we began by saying, the innermost shrine of human history, the " place " where man becomes most clearly conscious that life is a whole, and that he lacks some whole as distinct from this or that particular thing. And yet he never becomes fully conscious of this, because the history remains the history of religion. Otherwise religion would ultimately be compelled to reach out beyond itself and sacrifice itself, which could only happen if something should appear that was more than religion. And conversely, it is the distinctive mark of the mere history of religion that it never reaches a consciousness of the " crisis " of religion. Revelation is this crisis, overshadowing not merely man's spiritual life in general but particularly its very centre, religion. This crisis does not occur either in the legal consciousness of the highest forms of objective or theistic religion, nor again in mysticism. Both the legal pietist and the mystic are conscious of being hidden and safe in their religion. The crisis, the self-effacement of religion, occurs nowhere in the history of religion. That is the specific mark of Biblical revelation, which finds its completion in the crucifixion of the God-man by the most religious people in the world's history.

But it follows that what occurred then is the crisis not only of religion, but of all history. It is true that Jesus of Nazareth is a historical phenomenon, and his life a historical event. But as far as this goes it is no revelation of God. This appearance in history is the " incognito " of divine revelation, which can only be brought to light by faith—and that means, by God Himself. The man who discerns God in that event, not merely as God can be discerned in any event, but as God can be discerned in that event alone, and sees it as the revelation of Himself, becomes contemporary with that event. And conversely, he can only discern God in that event by becoming its contemporary, only through the fact that the word which then was spoken in the past tense speaks now in the present tense. " No one can call Christ his Lord save through the Holy Ghost."

What that " event " signifies is not history, but the end of history, a return to the source of all history, " Ur-End-Geschichte " or both the prelude and the goal of history.

No doubt to the extent that this knowledge is gained, something is taking place also in history. This element of primordial history realized by faith sends its waves into history. The invisible community of those who recognize that Name as their own becomes a phenomenon visible in history, indeed, one of the greatest of historical potencies, the church, or Christendom as a historical edifice. Despite the fact that the believer knows the goal of history as conceived by faith, he differs from the mystic in not being independent of history. History and culture continue to be the ground on which he has to work out his faith, the stage for the *ecclesia militans*, the possibility of her intensive and extensive growth ; because the God-created, real world which, fallen as it is, is that which receives the promise of its redemption in Christ ; the man of action, having his arena in history, is he who is claimed by God as His property ; the historical church is the one which is certain of its completion in the Kingdom of God.

Thus then even faith and the church participate in the process of history, despite faith's relation to what lies beyond all history. But this process of history is not all of one tenour. There is a spiritual growth of man, and this lies at the base of all true progress. But that growth does not consist, as an optimistic dualism will construe it, in man's coming-to-himself in the sense of a gradual redemption, but a coming-to-himself of divided man, who awakens to his need of redemption and perceives that redemption can never originate within history itself. But the reverse process also occurs—a backward movement, a recoil from the truth through illusion or deadening. The inquiry how the share taken by historical realities, powers, and events is to be estimated in reference to this particular plus or minus is altogether different from the question of progress. It is possible that what all the world would call progress may really belong to the minus-side, while what all the world would call retrogression may belong to the plus-side. This " book of life " is open to the sight of God alone. The church, too, is placed in this " to and fro " of history, and takes part in each actively and passively. Hence the growth of God's Kingdom as affirmed by faith is secret or (so to speak) subterranean, just as the true church is the invisible church although, being a church, she is never without a visible embodiment. All that faith knows about her is that she never escapes from this " to and fro " till something happens that is no longer in the sphere of history.

Chapter 8

THE ELEMENT OF TRUTH IN ORTHODOXY : THE BIBLE AS THE WORD OF GOD

(a) BIBLE AND REVELATION

Christian faith is Bible faith. When a Christian speaks without qualification of God's revelation, what he means is Holy Scripture. That is the truth contained in the Scriptural orthodoxy of Protestantism. Thereby it holds firmly to the principle that distinguishes Christian faith from all rationalism (philosophical doctrines of God and revelation), from subjectivism (revelation through mystical experience of God), and from historicism (identification of revelation with history, particularly history of religion). It is because Christian theology is consciously bound up with this unique and concrete datum that it cannot submit to be ranked in or subordinated to any general philosophy of religion. Its main thesis runs : the knowledge of God is to be drawn from Scripture. But the knowledge of God is not a special form of knowledge belonging as a class to some more inclusive conception of knowledge. It is rather the knowledge of the basis of all truth, it is the ultimate significance behind every kind of knowledge. It follows that all knowledge finds its standard and criterion here no matter whether the knower is aware of this or not. We do not measure

God's word in Scripture by the standard of reason :
we measure reason and indeed all knowledge by God's
word in Scripture.

Orthodoxy maintains this general thesis as the
fundamental thesis of Christian faith, and rightly so.
But in her interpretation of the thesis she deviates from
true Christian faith as widely as the other three schools.
The immense difference between these two apparently
so similar conceptions of the authority of the Bible
has only been clearly realized through the disintegration which orthodoxy has suffered as a consequence
of the impact of modern science. This is not to say
that the distinction has only existed since the advent
of modern science. It has always been latent in the
Christian church : we have a clear theological formulation of it already in the Reformers' principle of
Scripture, although in the case of the Reformers both
principles, orthodox and " reformed ", are often active
side by side. It is only the development of science
since the Enlightenment that has made a final
and unmistakable distinction between them vitally
necessary for Christian faith.

The crucial opposition between the orthodox and
reformed doctrine of Scripture has been previously
set forth in the historical part of this work. For
orthodoxy, the Bible as a book is the divinely revealed
truth. It is thus á revealed thing or object. For
unperverted Christian faith, however, Scripture is
only revelation when conjoined with God's spirit in
the present. The *testimonium spiritus sancti* and the
clarity of God's word are one and the same thing. The
Scripture-principle is therefore a paradoxical unity of
autonomy and authority, of what is given and what is

not given. Faith is contact with the absolute, hidden God, who reveals Himself to us personally as real, i.e. in something real. The real thing is Scripture to the extent that it is the witness to the revelation of God in Jesus Christ. " Scripture is the cradle in which Christ lies " (Luther). Just as a sentence consists of many words but has only one meaning, so the revelation of God in Scripture in the Old and New Testaments, in law and Gospel, has only one meaning, Jesus Christ. *Christus rex et dominus scripturae* ("The king and lord of Scripture is Christ" Luther). " Search the Scriptures, because . . . these are they that testify of me " (John v, 39). It is this content that makes them the word of God : for Christ is the Word. They are not in themselves the revelation, but only so far as and because they have this meaning, just as the words that constitute a sentence are not true by themselves, but in virtue of their single common meaning in the sentence. Hence the Christian does not speak of the words, but the word, of God. But just as it takes many words to make a meaning clear to us, so it takes the varied material which is spread out before us in Holy Scripture effectively to convey to us the meaning of the one Word, Jesus Christ. It requires the Old Testament as well as the New, the epistles as well as the gospels, the " unauthentic " gospel of John as well as the " authentic " synoptic gospels. The knowledge that this unity runs through all Scripture, is the knowledge that faith gives us. It is not the unity of an idea, even an idea of Christ, but the unity signified by the revelation of the eternal divine Word in time, i.e. in Jesus Christ who was crucified and rose again. An *idea* can be detached from its original source. It is timeless, universally and always true. Christian faith on the other hand is concerned with the truth which we perceive as true for us, not in itself, in virtue of the bare idea, but only because God actually utters it : we are concerned with revelation where everything depends on its having happened. The meaning throughout is the man, Jesus of Nazareth, in his historical " contingency ", in his " servant-form ", the man born of woman and subject to the law, obedient even to death on the cross. Everything in Scripture points to this as the fulfilment of all preparatory, predictive revelation, i.e. it points to the Mediator at the " central point " of history. All the books of the Bible spell out this name ; whether helplessly or forcibly, stammeringly or clearly, they instruct us about this acted meaning, some pointing forward, others backward.

With the object of coming closer to modern feeling, the antithesis has been put forward that God's word is not Scripture itself, but is contained in Scripture. This proposition could conceivably be correct : but as almost always understood it is false. For the aim that lies behind it is to discriminate revelation from what is not revelation in Scripture by an *a priori* principle of selection, by a content that can be defined beforehand. But this simply cuts the nerve of the Christian belief in revelation. Here everything turns on the character of revelation as fact, a " contingent " fact not capable of being inferred or controlled by us in any way. The important thing is not merely what is written, but the fact that it is written, and that always means that it is given in an " accidental "

form and in " accidental " association with other
material, at an " accidental " point in space and time,
and in an " accidental ", limited, and finite form.
It depends on the credibility of the introductory
formula : Thus saith the Lord, whether the word
of the prophets really has something to say to us ;
i.e. whether it merely expresses a commonplace of
morality, or the pious, heartfelt wish of a hopeful
fancy, or whether it is an authoritative communication
and revelation of mystery. To faith a word that is
found in the Bible, and just because it is found there,
is different from a similar word in (say) Laotse or
Plato. For to faith it is not the idea only that is important, but of equal importance is the fact that the
idea has been given ; or rather faith is concerned
not with the idea, but with the concrete happening of
revelation, with an actual conversation of God with man.

Our attitude to Scripture then, so far as it is God's
word to us, is not like our attitude to other books
however religious, true, wise, or worthy of respect
they may be—even though in these books some
things may be said more beautifully or even more
truly. The reason is that faith is not concerned with
" many things ", but always with the one, and, in
order that this one may exist, it necessarily appears
in this " accidental " volume known as the Bible.
Thereby, it is *eo ipso* different from the " similar "
and better said thing.

In saying this, we have also implied that our attitude
to the individual words and facts of Scripture is
entirely different from that of the orthodox view.
" The cradle in which Christ lies " is not the same
thing as Christ Himself. The words of Scripture, which

serve to witness Christ to us, are not Christ Himself, despite the fact that we only know Him through these words. Taken by themselves they are human words. The Bible is human testimony about God, but through this human factor God bears witness to Himself. The crucifixion of Jesus may have been judicial murder : that does not prevent it from being the world's salvation. It resulted from the assertions of false witnesses, but in spite of this or rather just thereby it becomes for faith the truth above all other truth. And so with the Bible as a whole. It is full of errors, contradictions, and misleading views of various circumstances relating to man, nature, and history. It contains many contradictions in its report of the life of Jesus ; it is over-grown with legend, even in the New Testament. Some parts of it are written in very helpless, colloquial, and even faulty language, while others again rise to the level of the greatest works of literature. The former fact no more destroys than the latter increases the authority which Scripture exercises over faith. The word of God is able to sound out most clearly from the worst Greek—perhaps the language of John might be mentioned by way of example.

The distinction of a human from a divine side of Scripture is not only permissible—" if nothing else will do "—but without it faith in the Bible is impure and mixed with bibliolatry. It is just on its freedom to distinguish the human from the divine side (but never to separate them) that the peculiarity of Christian faith in the Bible depends, in contrast to all veneration of holy scriptures in other religions. All other holy scriptures are at the same time fetishes, books of magic—too often indeed even the Bible is thus misused—and this belongs to their essential character. It is a property of Christian faith that the Bible should not be so regarded. It is neither a book of oracles, nor a divine encyclopædia of infallible instruction on all possible and impossible subjects. When so used, it is alienated from its proper meaning and abused. As with the whole Biblical revelation of God incarnate, the saying, *finitum non est capax infiniti* (the finite cannot grasp the infinite) is in place here. We are conscious of a lack of congruity between the means and the content of revelation. The characteristic " style " of God's revelation is to avail itself of the form of a servant, to humilate itself deeply and suffer descent into earthly frailties, not to thrust itself on men's view with the pomp of heathen theophanies, but even in the act of revelation to let itself be sought for as something hidden. It is in keeping with God's choice of a small, insignificant, and uncouth people, and with His revelation of His profoundest mystery on the cross at Golgatha, that He gave us His word in a literary document which will give the critics, in the legitimate exercise of their task, enough to do for generations to come. Faith in the Bible does not exclude, but includes, criticism of the Bible.

(*b*) BIBLE AND HISTORY

To the critical historian as such, the Bible is an accidental unity, a collection of documents of the most varied kind, and so a quarry of building stone for the reconstruction of a general system of history. To him there is no such thing as a " Bible ", because what makes the Bible a unity for faith, has no existence for the man of science. On the contrary, he can only make use of these documents when he separates them from that " accidental " unity known as the canon, in order to fit every part into its proper place in a historical continuum. But what is this historical continuum ? Not merely a causal connection of events in space and time. In themselves, or as a mere cinematograph of the past, these events have no meaning. The historian needs yet another continuum besides space and time, and it is found in the analogy that exists between man and nature. In the continuum of space and time every meaningful word is a blind spot, for " meaning " is not a visible datum in space and time. But in the continuum of analogy the meaningful word is a bright spot. Just because it has a comprehensible meaning, it can be classified as a fact in history. But of course we must not be understood to assert that all events must fit into one or other of these two kinds of continuum. Something might occur that neither belongs to the causal series nor yet has meaning through analogy, and so does not admit of being classified in any continuum with the world of phenomena. Thus a " blind spot " (so to speak) would arise in both continua. Of course the historian is obliged by his working hypothesis, his method—which is his qualification as scientist— to endeavour to clear up this " blind spot ". But it would be unscientific prejudice on his part to assert beforehand that this " blind spot " cannot but admit of being illuminated : this would mean that for him there cannot be anything ultimately inconceivable or incomprehensible. If he makes any such assertion, he passes over from the ground of science to that of some definite system of metaphysics or speculation.

The historian who uses analogy to gain his understanding finds, e.g. that the documents of the Bible constitute examples of such " blind spots in the continuum ".   They are obviously put forward as having a meaning, and they lay claim to being true. Yet to the historian who works with the continuum of analogy they are partly or even wholly opposed to sense, i.e. they are " blind ".   He can nevertheless attempt to classify them in one continuum or the other. In other words, (a) he can try to explain them (e.g. in terms of the psychology of primitive people, or by the limitations attaching to a particular period, or as due to temporary psychical anomalies, etc.).   Alternatively, (b) he can try to make them comprehensible to himself by simply striking out what is opposed to sense, and tracing them back to some universal ideal truth, whether moral, religious, or metaphysical.   But a good historian will do neither without the greatest hesitation.   For neither can be done without violence. If then he is a sober-minded historian, he will acknowledge that he has now come up against a historical fact which apparently does not admit of being classified in either of his continua ; it is something that to him is " provisionally " or even " finally " enigmatic.   The better acquainted he is with the limits of all scientific knowledge, i.e. the more capable as a critical investigator, the more readily will he consent to suspend his judgment before anything that refuses to take its place under general analogies.   For as a critical historian he knows that in this capacity he has no method that gives him control over the structure of events, and that he must keep an open mind for such events as he can neither understand nor explain—if such there be.

Another general question is that which relates to the relation between historical certainty and the certainty of faith. Reconstruction of the past belongs to the realm of empirical knowledge which as such can never arrive at absolute certainty, but only probability. The farther we are from historical events, the more uncertain they are to us. Any historical judgment can only be provisional, since all historical assertions mutually condition one another, and therefore none by itself can be definitive for all time. Every historical verdict is thus a verdict subject to appeal, and on the understanding that it may be revised later. It goes without saying that this holds good also in regard to historical judgments on Biblical material.

At the same time, however, faith passes absolute judgments on this same Biblical material, and these have meaning only when they have absolute certainty. If faith were founded on the historical assertions of the historian, it would of course find itself involved in an intolerable self-contradiction, for it would have to assume the unconditional certainty of what was only provisionally and relatively certain. From this difficulty, unreflective theological rationalists, or rather rationalists attempting a philosophy of religion, have drawn the conclusion that the believer now finds himself obliged to get free from history in order not to be exposed in any way to this uncertainty. The presupposition that lies at the base of this conclusion is that the historical element is historical in the same sense to both the believer and the historian. But it is just this presupposition that faith denies. It claims to stand in an altogether unique relation to historical fact, viz. in a relation of contemporaneity or even of identity.   Such a relation can, however, only exist where history can be defined as " Urgeschichte " or primordial history, in the sense of the previous chapter. The fact that this conception is susceptible of misuse in discussing the claims of faith and of historical criticism is no disproof of its legitimacy.   If Jesus really is the Christ and if the same God who is revealed in him bears witness to Himself and to the revelation in the believer, then in these facts we have something which, to the historian on the one hand, is merely of relative certainty in the continuum of history, but which to the believer on the other hand, is of absolute certainty in quite a different connection.   The historian will only be on his guard that this argument shall not be introduced into a purely historical discussion, and that the view of history as " Urgeschichte " may only come into his consideration as on the border-line of his own task and competence.

If now we turn from problems of this general character to the most important individual problems which gather round the broad affirmation of faith regarding Scripture, perhaps the first is that of the unity of Scripture.   Since to the historian the Bible is not a whole, but a chance combination of pieces of literature, so too for him it lacks inner unity.   The assertion that the Old Testament as well as the New treats of Jesus Christ has simply no meaning for him. It is only faith that can discern the inner and material connection of the Old and New Testaments—I am not now speaking of their historical connection.   But if the historian does not manipulate or do violence to his material, but exercises a perspicacious and careful search for historical reality, he will notice at least the similarity of the structure of thought in the Old and New Testaments and the specific difference of this structure from the " rest of the history of religion ". For the peculiarity of the Old Testament, in so far as it is discernible to the historian as such, consists not in the individual religious or moral ideas taken by themselves, but in the remarkable conjunction of these individual elements.   He cannot regard the conjunction as accidental, because it is constantly recurrent and all-pervasive.

If the phrase " ethical monotheism " may be chosen as an approximate description of the essential character of the Old Testament faith in God, it will nevertheless be clear at once that it must have a meaning fundamentally different from what it bears when applied to such phenomena as the religion of Plato or Epictetus, or any moral religion of the Enlightenment.   For we are not concerned in the Old Testament with a universal morality associated with a pallid idea of God, as, e.g. in the case of Epictetus ;   nor with an ethic which is therefore conceived as fundamentally internal to man and the world ;   but with the will of God Himself, His covenant with men, His dominion.   The fundamental commandment that includes all others is now one that enjoins fear of God, hallowing of the divine name as made known by divine revelation alone.   The result is that God is personal in a wholly different sense from that in which this can be affirmed of the God of Epictetus or Plato :   He is not the soul of the world, not the supreme idea, nor the world-overseer of Deism, nor the $\pi\rho\hat{\omega}\tau o\nu$ $\kappa\iota\nu o\hat{\upsilon}\nu$ of Aristotle,   but the Lord of the world and of history. He governs His creation in an incomprehensible fashion, just as He called it into being incomprehensibly by His word ; and He is revealed as the incomprehensible ruler by His living intervention in action and speech. All analogies with ethical monotheism fade away completely when we observe that this dreadful, holy, angry God, the Ruler and the Judge, is at the same time a merciful Father, who dwells with those who have a broken heart, those who know that none living is justified in His sight ; that He is ever drawing the unfaithful back to Himself ; that He purposes to reinstate the wicked world which He once created good ; that His whole work, in anger and clemency, judgment and redemption, law and promise, always came under the same point of view, viz. that of a covenant of God with men to restore the sole dominion of God, which has been obscured by men's dis-obedience.

And these contents, rendered paradoxical throughout by the strange combinations, are not given as the result of man's effort to acquire knowledge, nor yet as universal truth which comes home immediately to everyone, nor again as *sensus communis* (common sense). Rather even the moral law itself is given by a free, sovereign act of divine revelation, as a thing unattainable by human kind and brought down to them from Sinai's top after the lonely meeting between God and His intermediary, Moses ; as a free gift, in which God makes known at once His remoteness and His nearness, His mercy and His dreadful sternness. The special form wherein this special content is given is the prophet, the man of God elect as mediator between God and man. The prophets are not *homines religiosi* (religious geniuses) in the sense in which the science of comparative religion uses the term, nor saints, nor patterns of religion venerated by the people, nor ascetics who practise and teach the *via religiosa* (way of religion), nor seekers after God who pursue and cultivate a special intercourse with God, special and exceptional experiences of God. They are on the contrary men who against their own will are taken by God into special service. They are only men whom He uses and uses up, men who do not attract anyone to them or ask anyone either to imitate or venerate them. They are impersonal channels of God's word as it utters His demands and promises, men who are wholly devoted to the delivery of the word, and so discharge their commission to the world. It is not themselves, nor their religious life, of which indeed as a rule we know as good as nothing, but the objective word of God to the world, that passes through them into history.

This truth alone will enable us to understand that most remarkable chapter where the whole meaning of the Old Testament is concentrated. This meaning lies in the covenant of God with men, which, however, does not admit any relation of partnership ; the judgment of God, which at the same time sets men right ; the mediator of the word, who gives himself over wholly to God's work for mankind, and yet in whom God really gives Himself over to men. It is the chapter dealing with the suffering servant of God (Isaiah, liii), the prophecy of the unconditionally obedient man who gives his life as an offering for sin, though himself perfectly righteous. The material that the modern historical school of exposition has adduced to explain this culminating point of Old Testament teaching proves utterly inadequate for comprehending it. Granting that we may assume the servant of God to be the people of Israel, nevertheless it is in no way the actual people of history, but an object which cannot be comprehended by means of any pragmatic conception. The primary subject of this chapter is God Himself. Everything that happens takes place by His grace and otherwise must appear as a wrong done to one who is without guilt. We stand in the immediate presence of revelation, where expiation for sin and divine forgiveness, God's word and God's act, judgment and promise, are identical both in the word which is the full personal presence of God, and in that historic reality, which is altogether and solely the word of God—Jesus Christ.

Of course the historian is in a position to adduce parallels from other religions to almost every important separate feature of the Old Testament. But only the crassest materialist confuses the symbol with the symbolized, or can overlook the fact that the entirely different context, the paradoxical context in which everything found elsewhere appears in the Old Testament, gives a wholly different meaning such as does *not* occur otherwise. The mere historian can only stand there and shake his head, as one who does not understand, when he is brought face to face with this meaning, but, if he has any insight at all, he cannot deny its different quality as against everything else with which he is acquainted. Perhaps he will ascertain with astonishment that as a matter of fact this very paradox of unity of meaning, which comes forward ever more plainly in the Old Testament, is completed in the New Testament, and that all the lines which began in the former meet in the latter at a single point. Behind this unity which the believer can yet discover despite its strangeness, although he cannot prove it, he recognizes the one witness to the revelation of God in Jesus Christ who no longer merely speaks, but is, the Word ; who no longer merely preaches, but grants forgiveness ; who does not merely proclaim the Kingdom of God, but embodies it and brings it about.

The case is similar in regard to the unity of the New Testament. Here again the historian will distinguish, as he has good right to do, the different types of teaching, say, the synoptic, Pauline, and Johannine. But if he is sufficiently impartial and clear sighted, he cannot help perceiving here also the traces of a constantly recurrent, unifying structure which he cannot construe under causation or analogy. All the writings of the New Testament, the earliest as well as the latest, the synoptists and the rest, testify with one accord that this man, Jesus of Nazareth, is the Christ, the " Lord " ; he who introduces the turning-point in the world's history for judgment and salvation, and whose coming again will signify the end of the age. All differences vanish before this fundamental unity. Why should not what is incomprehensible be expressed in different ways ? Is it surprising that the community of Christians required time before they were clear as to the meaning of the tremendous event that had befallen them ? After all, the simple prayer of *Maranatha*, Come, Lord (Jesus)—

which, as may obviously be deduced from the preserva-
tion of the Aramaic word in tradition, was used even
by Jewish Christians, i.e. by men who were familiar
with the first commandment—already said everything
to which the boldest formulæ of the Nicene and
Chalcedonian creeds gave fixed expression in forms of
abstract thought.

We cannot prevent the historian attempting to
penetrate behind even the earliest tradition of the
church, in order to gain as faithful a picture of Jesus
as possible. This attempt, which was formerly under-
taken very confidently but to-day only with great
reserve, has little significance for theology. For there
are two things that must be evident to the historian :
(1) that the primary historical datum is not a life of
Jesus such as secular history can turn to account, but
the church's witness to Christ, and that as a historian
he makes of these sources something entirely different
from the aim of the sources themselves ; (2) that his
undertaking, however it may turn out, cannot decide
the question that concerns faith, viz. who was Jesus ?
Assuming that a reconstruction of the historical
picture without any blanks led to our realizing that
Jesus really did say nothing about his Messiahship
or his crucial significance for the relation between
God and man, nothing about the significance of his
suffering and death, in regard to the revelation and
work of God ; still the testimony of the apostles and
the faith founded thereon would remain unaffected.
Who is prepared to establish the *conditiones sine
qua non* (indispensable conditions) of the historical
appearance of the Redeemer, and of his activity and
teaching ?   Why should not one whose historical

appearance was only (!) that of a prophet, *be* the Son
of God and the Redeemer, and his life and death be
the divine act which surpasses all prophecy to the
same degree as a fulfilment surpasses a promise ?

The historian may be able to reconstruct the picture
of Jesus up to a certain point : but he cannot make
out anything of the meaning, or the spiritual reality
of this picture. E.g. if Jesus was really the Christ, why
should he anticipate in his word what was to happen
and thus strip the event of its reality ? Why should
he betray the incognito of his Messiahship when
after all everything turned on its not becoming a matter
of theory but remaining a matter of personal decision ?
Is it very surprising that the " historical Jesus " speaks
in very different fashion from the witnesses of his cross
and passion ?

Of course it remains free to anyone (quite humanly
speaking) to hold by this picture of Jesus and reject
the witness of the primitive church. Only let him be
aware that the picture in virtue of which he makes
his decision is an integral part of that witness which
he rejects ; that there never was a Christian church
that knew Jesus as anything but the " object " of faith
and preaching, as the Lord who, in contrast with all
other men, stands at the side of God : not one of the
redeemed, but the Redeemer ; not judged along with
men, but judge ; not joining them in prayer, but
himself addressed in prayer, and that it is just by these
facts and these alone that the Christian church is
distinguished, then and always, from other religious
societies.

But we have already conceded more than we should.
The historical appearance of Jesus, as traceable behind

the witness of the primitive church, cannot be fitted, without involving ambiguity, into any analogical scheme at the disposal of the historian. There are two theories that are irreconcilably opposed to each other : the first sees in Jesus a prophet who taught a " lofty, pure, moral type of religion ", who conceived his divine commission in terms of this sort of preaching. This is the Jesus who, according to Wellhausen, represented himself under the figure of the sower, tranquilly scattering the divine seed over the earth. The second theory is the eschatological, which interprets all his doings and sayings as " acts of his Messianic consciousness ", the expression of what Schweitzer calls his " dogmatic " claim to Messiahship :   this claim is incomprehensible to us, and relates to the miraculous coming of the Messianic Kingdom. For the former conception, the Messianic and eschatological element either remains unintelligible, or else its meaning is wholly transformed. Hence this school tries to strike it out of the picture of Jesus as a later theology of the church, or else as a secondary and unimportant feature of the portrait. In the latter view, the moral sublimity and repose that appear in Jesus, so free from anything like fanaticism, remain inexplicable. So also does another fact that the secular historian cannot deny, viz. the whole of the tremendous content of his preaching. Both contrast only too sharply with the fantastic dogmatism of the eschatological school. The actual content of the tradition can only be purged of this contradiction by doing it great violence. To the historian, not only Jesus, but the origin of primitive Christianity, and the faith in Christ and his resurrection, remain a riddle, an "blind spot" in the continuum, and this can only be explained away by arbitrary manipulations, or transformed into something analogous by dull psychological devices. What comes between us and the evidence of the New Testament is not in the least the fruits of critical investigation, as is so often asserted, but merely the trend of modern man's thought. On the contrary, it is rather the case that the historian is tempted to decide in favour of the Christian faith (were that possible) simply in order to reach at last the solution of a problem that can be dealt with in no other way.

In the last place, let us look at a problem which has occupied the foreground in most recent times—the " explanation derived from the history of religion ". It is an undeniable fact that, like other men, the New Testament writers expressed themselves in the language of their day. On this fact it has been thought admissible to build the theory that the essential contents of the New Testament can be explained from the world of Hellenistic, late-Jewish, and gnostic religion. It is in keeping with the general positivism, or theory of cause and effect, which is characteristic of our time, that some have obviously ventured to draw the conclusion from the *post hoc* to the *propter hoc* without more ado, not suspecting that the significant utterance of an independent thinker never has its basis, but at most its occasion, in his " environment ". But this false conclusion is specially mischievous when only the words, or the stock of ideas, are identical, but not the meaning, i.e. the inner coherence. To a theory of verbal inspiration such genealogies of words and individual ideas might of course be fatal. Once for all a death-blow has now been given to the theory of a " Greek of the Holy Ghost ", as also to the mechanical theory of inspiration. It is not of such theories that we are now speaking. But the extravagant value set upon such parallels from the history of religion can be discounted by the simple truth that words and stocks of ideas are related to meaning in much the same way as colours and canvas are to a painting. The same materials are employed by the bungler and the master ; what makes the difference between them is the thing that they " express by these means ", i.e. the unifying sense which the words and ideas are constrained to serve, and this sense again is made plain in the " structure " of the stock of ideas. Only a crass materialism confuses the two with each other ; but it must of course be allowed that the structure that reveals the meaning cannot be manipulated so easily as the stock of ideas by means of a scientific technique. Anyone who has once come to know the fundamental difference between the structure seen in Biblical thought and that of all other phenomena in the history of religion (see the previous chapter) will expect from such explanations only second-rate in-struction—not however to be despised on that account. The fact of having material in common will but be felt as less and less crucial, to have less and less crucial significance, the more highly (in the language of history) the originality of the peculiar structure is valued. That this originality reaches its maximum in the Biblical circle of thought will not be questioned by any sober historian, whatever may be his attitude to Christianity in other respects.

Jesus, primitive Christianity, and the prophetic

religion of Israel must still be " phenomena of a fundamentally enigmatic nature " (Overbeck) even to a secular historian who has insight.   The Bible would not be the word of God if the position were otherwise, either positively or negatively, i.e. if we could actually explain it completely as a human production, or if we were actually driven to recognize that it is something more than that.   It is the word of God precisely in virtue of the fact that it reserves to faith the verdict that it is the word of God ;   and in virtue of the further fact that because faith is what it is it can recognize God's revelation in Scripture, or rather must recognize it when God grants such recognition.

(c) The Bible and the Scientific View of the World

The first thrust against the orthodox conception of the Bible came not from the side of " history " but of natural science.   Modern astro-physics, geography, and geology have once for all destroyed the view of the world characteristic of antiquity and the Bible. The conflict of orthodoxy with modern science, which is still carried on here and there, means nothing more from the standpoint of Christian faith than a superflous protraction of that period of unworthy apologetic devices which viewed as a whole now lies behind us. A fruit of these past controversies may be seen in the revived consideration of the relation between affirmations of faith and those sciences that are concerned with matters belonging to the world of space and time.   By its undreamed of progress science has forced faith to disencumber itself of certain relics of (primitive) science, with the object not of " confining itself to its own domain "—for this domain includes all existence —but of becoming clearer as to the nature and mode of its relation to the existing world.

The investigation of things and events in space and time as such is the business of science alone : where such matters are under discussion, it is not for faith to intervene even in the framing of scientific hypotheses, on which, of course, all scientific progress depends. In particular, it is the most dubious of all the devices of theological apologetics to settle down by preference in the gaps of scientific theory. Thus it should never have entered the head of Christian theologians to intervene in the controversy over Darwinism, so long as the framing of evolutionary theories was confined in a strictly scientific manner to the domain of what is really open to observation or, in other words, to past events in space and time. The difficulty of framing valid hypotheses concerning the events of the far past is no real obstacle to the ultimate legitimacy of the attempt, and certainly furnishes no occasion for the intervention of theologians.   Conversely, we ought by this time to be allowed to ask that men of science should recognize that even in their field problems arise with which science is only partially if at all competent to deal, such as (e.g.) the rise of form and of final causes ; in a word, the problem of origin (*vide supra*, p. 121). The investigation of nature, too, meets with limits to scientific research in the shape of " primordial phenomena ", with regard to which the means at the disposal of the natural sciences are the least valuable of any for making progress.

Once these fundamental distinctions have been made, it immediately becomes clear how impossible it is that any essential position of Christian faith should be affected sympathetically by changes in the scientific view of the world. E.g. it is extremely naïve to believe that the Copernican theory has expelled man from that central position in the universe which is assigned him by the Christian belief in creation and redemption. The essential attitude on this point might have been learnt from Kant who, one may say, estimated and described his own contribution to philosophy as getting rid of that of Copernicus. The view that modern anthropology has disposed of the Christian doctrine of the original state and the Fall (in Adam) is as superficial as that jest of Laplace's, that even with his best telescope he had been unable to discover any God in heaven. Of course, it is necessary to free the substance of the Bible from its temporary forms, coming as these often do from primitive science or mythology, although this does not mean replacing them by modern ideas. This task has already been silently fulfilled with reference to the idea of heaven, but it does not really belong to the great problems of theology. The difficulties which theology has to overcome are practical and educational rather than scientific. The conflict between faith and science has never been serious nor one that affected central questions. It is with philosophy that the serious conflict of faith is fought out. There is no opposition between faith and knowledge, but between faith and the autonomy of reason, between the actual and the purely theoretic attitude of man to his life and to history.

Thus the real opponent is not science but a false

estimate of science, a scientific monism, i.e. the superstitious belief in one science including all possible forms of knowledge in itself. Any well-considered methodology or criticism of knowledge would suffice to make clear the illicit character of such scientific monism. Even to the critical man of science reality appears to consist of degrees or strata, only one of which is the subject-matter of a particular fundamental science. By their nature the phenomena of life rise above the science of physics, those of consciousness above biology, those associated with spiritual values or normativity above psychology. The higher grade of the moment, when observable among the facts of the lower, makes a " blind spot " in the latter's continuum. The physicist as such does not know what to do with the conception of an organism, although organisms enter into the domain of physics. The psychologist experiences a like embarrassment in regard to the conception of freedom : and so on. The whole of the existing world may be thought of as a series of concentric circles ; within the widest of them lies all that is—in the sense of definite existence —while within the inmost there is only the reasonable being, man. The discrimination of separate circles does not conflict with the continuity of the world of existence as conceived especially by the modern man, provided we recognize that this continuity has only one side and is not reversible. A point can only be understood as the limit of a straight line, the straight line only as the limit of a surface, rest only as the limit of movement, death only as the limit of life, and what is psychical only as the limit of what is spiritual. But the mode of understanding is not convertible, The modern doctrine of evolution has done a good deal towards obscuring the nonconvertibility by turning the *post hoc* into a *propter hoc*. Thereby it has brought great confusion into the whole system of scientific thought. The world is suffering to-day from this confusion and it hampers also the discussion of the problems of theology and philosophy of religion.

It would, for instance, mean a great advance in the critical study of the Bible if the above-mentioned grading of the sciences were to receive more or less general recognition, or —what comes to the same thing—if at last the superstition of a scientific monism were to vanish. It would then be recognized that when the Bible is viewed in turn from the level of the various stages of historical science it discloses wholly different strata of its significance. The positivist sees in it that it provides instances of conformity to sociological laws, the humanist or idealist—e.g. Herder—only that it unfolds the splendours of the human soul. A man who takes his stand upon a universal " religion " (" essence of religion ") will recover from it the rudiments of all religions. They may all be right. The only question is whether, beyond them all, there is not yet another science, one that investigates the Bible starting from the presuppositions of the Bible itself, i.e. from the point of view of a special revelation. It would be a science of Biblical theology, as distinguished from the science of religion. It would use the same scientific criterion as all other sciences, viz. the carrying out of its own principle according to strict method. It is prejudice created by scientific monism that still leads many people to refuse to allow the scientific right of such a theological science. At bottom this is the same narrowness as that shown by positivism, when it denies independence to the mental as compared with the natural sciences.

The recognition of strata of reality and the corresponding gradation of the sciences has, of course, in the main, only negative significance for the central problem of theology, which is revelation : thus a host of sham problems can be cleared out of the way. But the very nature of revelation involves a twofold attitude to this, as to all other instances of rational knowledge. On the one hand, revelation appears as, so to speak, the summit of the whole system of gradation : revelation is the narrowest of the various circles, and within it is to be found not human beings as such, but only one *humanus*, the God-man. Knowledge of the self-revealing God is thus the highest knowledge, including in itself all other forms of knowledge. That is the picture of being and knowledge presented by medieval theology, and pre-eminently by Thomism. Revelation is reason in the proper sense, and theology science in the proper sense. That view is clearly the obverse of the modern naturalist doctrine of evolution. And, as we have seen, it is not false. It has entirely in its favour the truth that Christ is the fulfilment of the law, and that revelation is the fulfilment alike of nature and of humanity. But it is one sided and " undialectic ", and in this respect is false.

For revelation is not related to the truth about nature only as fulfilment ; to mention only one point, it is not merely the climax in which the truths of all religions find their unity and completion. The interval between Christ and (what one might call) the superlatively rational man is not only a minimum, but at the same time a maximum, because here sin becomes an actual fact. S. Thomas's phrase : *Gratia non tollit naturam, sed perficit* (grace does not set aside, but completes, nature) has against it all that revelation means by dying, conversion, return to God, rebirth, new creation. The whole law of successive degrees is overturned by the single utterance, " Except ye turn, and become as children. . . ." The upper takes the lower place, and the lower the upper. The sinful publican is nearer to God than the blameless Pharisee, infants and fools than the great and wise. The very law of successive degrees, i.e. of continuous approxima- tion, is that against which divine revelation is primarily directed because it imperils the sovereignty of God, the distinction between creature and Creator, the absolutely unique relation between God and all else that exists. It imperils the recognition that there is no continuity to bridge the gulf between created and Creator, between human action and divine creation and redemption. That continuity is established only by God, who destines all things to Himself : but this God also reserves His unique character to Himself, and severs all continuity between Himself and His creation, and so too, between His self-revelation and all the forms of human knowledge. It follows that the vindication of divine revelation which is the task of theology, this " science " together with the Scriptures, which are its foundation, will always issue in an ultimate opposition to every other kind of knowledge, although this latter neither can nor should be obviated. If this were not the case, we should have in the last analysis a theoretic show of truth in which responsible decision or the venture of faith would be submerged, a supernatural theory after the manner of a universal speculative truth, which would deprive the individual of his responsibility for exercising faith.

The orthodox doctrine of the Bible is a truth of this kind. It confers a theoretically universal character upon something that only becomes divinely true

M

through our being actually addressed by God. The truth of revelation changes from a judgment as to actual existence to an *a priori* judgment. With the universality of a law the attribute " divinely true " is ascribed beforehand to the entire content of the Bible. Herein lies the essence of the orthodox doctrine of verbal inspiration. It spells the death of any living faith in the Bible. That is not the way in which the Reformers, nor yet genuine Christian faith, ever read the Bible even in the age of orthodoxy. Like other false thoughts, the orthodox theory may overlay genuine faith without necessarily extinguishing it. Wherever devout Christians have read the Bible, they have read it seriously, i.e. for what God says to them personally.

(*d*) THE BIBLE AS CANON

The result of our discussion is that there neither can nor should be any criterion of divine revelation assignable beforehand. Even Luther's " right touchstone for censuring Scripture ", his much-invoked principle : " Whatever sets Christ forth is apostolic," was not intended in itself to be a prescribed principle. It only aims at characterizing the inner connection or unity of meaning common to all revealed truths. For of course it is also an element of faith that the connecting link of the words, the Word in the words, belongs of necessity to the revealed truth itself : it is a universal Reformation principle that the Bible is to be expounded according to the *analogia fidei* (analogy of . faith), i.e. in accordance with its own internal connection. But this connection can be grasped only within the sphere of faith ; it is a connection learned by practice in the school of faith, and not cognizable beforehand by means of theoretic logic. What has its connection in faith and in revelation can only be discerned by faith, just as the connection between truths of reason depends on the proof of this connection and so can only be grasped by being thought out.

Consequently, as faith is not in a position, by using some principle, to determine beforehand the scope of the revelation contained in Scripture, it regards this scope as a contingent datum, without however making the generalization characteristic of orthodoxy, i.e. without asserting a universal rule that whatever comes within that scope is the word of God. In this way we reach a proper conception of the canon. The canon is a determination of revealed truth and it is as perilous as it is necessary. Perilous, because it specially exposes us to the menace of orthodox misunderstanding ; but unavoidable, because only so can we take revelation seriously as a thing given in an individual event. Bible faith will have to prove its vitality by its power of maintaining faith in the canon simultaneously with the necessity for Biblical criticism.

The central truth of Christian faith is that an event of decisive and eternal significance took place at a single point in the historical world of space and time. That is why it is called *Christian* faith. For this reason Jesus Christ is the main subject of all Christian preaching, and accordingly of all theology. Its first duty is to speak of the two great themes of incarnation and reconciliation—that in Christ the Eternal Word became flesh, and that the word of reconciliation was spoken by God Himself. This central content of faith is what determines the specific character of all its other affirmations. And a further consequence of the connection of revelation with a point in time is that the Bible, as the evidence of that event, becomes the standard and source of Christian knowledge. These two central points are really only one, viz. Christ in the Scripture : they are the main subject of Christian doctrine and also the presupposition of a " philosophy of religion " consonant with Christian theology.

If it is not the business of dogmatic theology in the proper sense, still less is it that of a " Protestant philosophy of religion " to develop a " system ". Its sole business is to give such an account of the Christian meaning of the words revelation and faith, which are also in use beyond the Christian pale, as firstly, to distinguish them clearly from every other use of them, and secondly, to make it clear that revelation, as something grasped by faith, is the answer to the grand question of man's life as this finds expression in his spiritual quest and his religion. The fact that from the standpoint of Christian faith all questions are shown to point in one direction and to find their answer in one word might indeed create the appearance of a system. But this seeming " systematic theology " is only a simple recognition on the part of faith that God Himself is the judge of all thoughts and the saviour in every need. If we had at our disposal an idea of God, i.e. a principle in which all our questions could find their solution, Christian theology would be only a hyper-dialectical brand of Hegelianism. But precisely at this point the purely negative character of this " system " comes to light : it has not any such solving principle at its disposal. On the contrary, it consists in constantly referring at every point to the reality of the revelation and the crucial character of faith itself. In neither case can the burden of responsibility be at all lessened by any general principle—which means also, by any process of theological thought. All the " solutions " which a true theology offers are always the same, and this one solution can only be recognized as being what it is by him who himself makes the decision of faith, and only in as far as he makes it.

Grisebach, from whose thought theology has still a good deal to learn, stresses the unreality of a dialectical theology, in his criticism of Kierkegaard (*Grenzen des Erziehers*). On this matter—as in others too—it seems to me that he overlooks the fact that all human speech is necessarily " unreal ", because sinful men never stand concretely in an " I and thou " relation with God. When he writes such a sentence as " It is only when self-contradictory man is controlled that the Eternal is mirrored " he himself erects a system, of a Neoplatonic type, which is perhaps more dangerous than any dialectical theology concerned to abrogate self, a theology that has observed that in our existence there is no " real action " any more than real speech, unless it be of divine grace.

Since our solution is such only for faith, it is granted only on the terms that it has constantly to take its rise from the problem of life. This is the secret of its reality. The Reformation started when Luther saw that repentance has to be repeated daily. Seeing this meant that all intellectualism in theology was uprooted. The " solution " realized by faith only exists where the contradiction in human life is vitally grasped in all its fullness, i.e. as a contradiction existing not simply in theory, but in ultimate fact ; and where the truth of divine revelation is constantly wrested by passionate faith from the contradiction between reason and the inward verdict of conscience. Since, however, we are here concerned with a datum, the solution cannot lay claim to any originality. It can be no more than a commentary, as timely as possible, on the " philosophy of religion " that Paul formulated for the first time, but in a permanently classic manner, in the second chapter of his first epistle to the Corinthians.

BIBLE REVELATION AND THE MAN OF TO-DAY

Science, philosophy, and culture are man's creations. Hence man himself is the problem of all problems and the greatest of all riddles. It is a characteristic of the man of to-day that he is not aware of this self-evident truth. He makes himself a part of his own science, whereas science is really a part of his own real self. Opposition to faith in revelation does not grow out of science, philosophy, or culture, but out of false thinking about science, philosophy, and culture. It is the " isms " that are the enemies of faith. Behind every " ism " there stands a faith, and one too that makes a " whole out of a part ", an absolute out of a relative—not merely conceiving, but at the same time ordaining. Every " ism " is a case of surrender to something subordinate as though it were absolute. " Isms " are thus idols. It follows that the controversy of faith with the " isms ", which is the task of theology, is a conflict with idolatry.

Hence, an objective, neutral, or " purely scientific " theology is a monstrosity. For genuine theology, theology that knows its business, is always born of the passion of faith. Accordingly it is always in the nature of a personal conflict ; it is always likewise personal confession. Its subject-matter is of such a kind that it can only be fittingly dealt with in a personal way. It is part of the task of the church, i.e. a part of the conflict of the *ecclesia militans* (church militant). To this extent the theological faculties remain outside the *universitas scientiarum* (circle of the sciences). If they still find toleration inside the universities, this may be taken as a sign that the cultured man of to-day is still conscious that science can only remain healthy as long as it is aware of being founded on something that exceeds science. Thus the existence of theological faculties within the borders of university activity, when viewed from this standpoint, affords a proof of a critical consciousness on the part of the cultured society that pursues the sciences. But the result is that no theology justifies its existence there unless it takes note of this antithesis and gives it clear expression. Theology in the guise of an objectively neutral science of religion is a contradiction in terms.

It is the special business of that part of theology which we have designated " philosophy of religion " to manifest the opposition between the " isms " of the men of any given period on the one hand and revelation on the other, not with the object of reaching an objective scientific view, but solely with the practical religious aim determined by the church's activities. Even on its general side, as philosophy of religion, theology is altogether a church science. Not of course in the sense that it takes over from the church a complete dogma merely to give it formal elaboration— that is the corrupt conception of its task fathered by historicism—but in the sense that by commission from the church it gives abstract consideration to the presuppositions involved in the formation of theological conceptions, i.e. a consideration of revelation as distinct from reason, and this on the basis of the standard furnished by faith.

The opposition between theology and the " isms " of the man of to-day depends precisely on this fundamental reference to Bible and church. For if anything is characteristic of the quality peculiar to present-day man, it is the refusal to recognize the association that finds expression in the words " ecclesiastical " or " Biblical ". The blame for this situation belongs not solely to the modern emancipation of reason and culture or to modern education, but equally to the church herself in virtue of a false conception of herself and her standard, the Bible. The terrible features of clericalism and orthodoxy have become so deeply impressed on the memory of western peoples that, for the time being and in wide circles, it is impossible to obtain so much as a quiet hearing for the interpretation of itself in its theology which Christianity offers. When earlier in our discussion we put orthodoxy on a level with rationalism and other " isms " we thereby gave expression to our opinion that it should be regarded as an " ism ".

Indeed, we must now go a step further. The " men of to-day ", whose idols serve as rivals to revelation, include all of us ; and the idols are ours, i.e. those of the theologians and the churches. Revelation and church are not opposed to the idols of some people, but of all. There are no shelters that secure us from this attack, whether they be churches or theological faculties. On the contrary they are just the positions most liable to attack on the whole human front. Our consideration of the meaning of revelation in the service of the church lacks thoroughness and insight if it fails to recognize this very point. For every theology is in danger of becoming an orthodoxy, and every church is full of clerical tendencies. There is orthodoxy wherever living faith stiffens into a settled system of belief, i.e. into a false objectifying of faith. By so doing, theological knowledge takes its stand on the ground where there are assured human positions that are fixed absolutely. An orthodoxy like that is not a hair better than the most hopeless relativity, and the controversy with it is ordained by God. Similarly, where a church takes up a position towards the outside world as the church in possession, having command of what can help the world, be it in the medieval and hierarchical, or modern and humanitarian sense, the church is *ipso facto* degraded into a worldly power and therefore becomes the opposite of its true purport. The church's only " possession " is the word : but possession of the word of God means at the same time the knowledge that it rests with God's free grace all the time to give or to withhold.

Thus it cannot be a question of spheres that may be marked off within the world when we refer to the Bible and the church in order to contrast the kind of reflexion that is the task of theology with the rest of human activity. When this reflection is rightly conducted, it must make anyone who takes part in the task most painfully conscious that he himself belongs to the " men of to-day ". The Bible and the church are not simply given entities. Their universal claim depends precisely on the fact that they are not, and just for this reason they involve a reckoning for every man and every entity that would assert its own rights.

Only because the revelation which we have in mind when we refer to Bible and church pronounces judgment on every theology and church, and likewise every other phenomenon of human history, can it really be the divine element that is superior to all human things. But we are not in a position to say this, unless and in so far as we know of Him for whose sake theology and church exist.

The first judgment pronounced by revelation has reference to theologies and churches ; and only the second to the world and secular idolatries.

Further, the assault is directed against the idols of science, philosophy, and culture, and not against science, philosophy, and culture in themselves. Rightly understood there is no problem of reason and revelation. It is not reason that is opposed to revelation, but man's pride in his rationality, science, philosophy, and culture. The very man who makes serious work with reason has some perception of this. He becomes critical and condemns a non-critical reason as shallow and frivolous.

But he cannot be truly critical by reason alone, since within its limits he cannot penetrate the character of evil, but is bound to underestimate evil, by holding fast to mere reason and letting it suffice him. The real opponent of faith is not the knowledge and culture that man has worked out for himself through the centuries, but the failure and the reluctance to see the insufficiency of these achievements. The mere idea of culture and knowledge, if taken seriously, would lead to a perception of their limitations. To use the language of faith, it would of itself " lead to repentance ", at least in as far as it would deprive the

rational man of any rational ground for opposing
revelation. In his critical capacity a man *can* of course
oppose revelation—otherwise the basis of faith would
lie not in revelation but critical reflection. Nevertheless he cannot do so on grounds of reason but only by
transgressing the bounds set by the very idea of
reason. What it all means then is that our attitude to
the demand for faith is not a matter of reason, whether
positive or negative, but of personal decision. The
value of critical reflection lies in the fact that it
necessitates personal decision.

Accordingly it is not correct to say that the development of our knowledge makes faith difficult. It
makes faith easier at the same time as it makes it
difficult. Faith is easier as well as harder for a man
than for a child. Conversely, its connection with
theology and church (in their empirical sense) makes faith
not only easier, but also harder. Faith is more difficult
for none than for the theologian, and for none is it
harder to be a Christian than for the baptized. The
reason is that there is no temptation so great as the
temptation to put a theological system in the place
of faith, and membership of the visible church in
place of being a Christian.

The " man of to-day " is at bottom always the same.
For man's self-confidence in his possession of reason
and culture (or in his theological or ecclesiastical
possessions) is always the same. On the other hand,
the man of to-day is also constantly different, in the
sense that the form of his self-confidence constantly
varies. Faith and accordingly theology, which should
be servant of the former, always have to do with the
man of the present. Accordingly when they enter

into controversy with secular thought they must always keep to the forms in which that unvarying self-confidence of man's finds expression at the moment. Hence theology is bound to look quite different at various times although ultimately it has always to do with the same problems and the same truth. That is why we have allowed our problem to be set us by history, for it puts before our eyes the " isms " that are dominant to-day : these we have discussed in the foregoing pages. The only duty left to us in conclusion is to point out that all those (four) tendencies of thought are so many forms of man's self-assertion against the truth of revelation, in other words, so many forms of unbelief, to the extent that they assert themselves absolutely, i.e. that men stand out thereby against revelation.

Even the believer can be a relativist : he can, and indeed must, and this to an extent to which no other can be. But what he cannot be is a mere realistic sceptic. He sees at the same time the superior right of idealism, of the idea, to relativism. As a believer, however, he knows that both scepticism and idealism can never make peace with each other, because each is in the right against the other. Thus the believer sees too the relative right of the cynic to deny culture and of the romantic to deny law, but equally the superior right of aiming at culture and seriously pursuing it. This aim and pursuit are supported by the idea of control by the spirit, and all the more where human personality and freedom appear as the central interest of culture. At the same time he sees that, as a system, scepticism in regard to culture is an enormity, but that culture if treated as the final

arbiter of human life lacks contact with reality and
final seriousness. He sees how man's life in past and
present has fluctuated between a false pride in
reason and a false self-repudiation, between cynicism
and pursuit of illusions, and he knows that anything
besides this see-saw is impossible within the sphere
of the " natural man ".

But faith means abandoning this sphere or rather
being put in another. " Our citizenship," says Paul,
" is in heaven." The believer therefore knows that
the " citizenship " of Plato and all his idealist successors
is an illusion ; and equally that a church-state, or a
culture under church direction, is a superstition. But,
as faith is not sight, and as in faith we only overcome
the contradiction that trammels human existence if
at the same time we endure it, if we persist in it " in
the body ", for this reason the believer does not with-
draw from a rational life that aims at knowledge and
culture. He takes his part in them, they furnish the
material of the activity by which he has to prove
himself as a Christian, a member of the *ecclesia militans*.
Aware of their infirmity he does so without cynicism
or illusion, seriously, but only with such a seriousness
as has behind it the primary seriousness of life. He
gives himself to the tasks they set him, but only in
such a way that the task he primarily intends is not
these, but the task to which he has put his hand in
faith, and which by its nature can never enter directly
into his work. He leads an indirect life as *homo viator*,
a pilgrim who does not confuse harbour with home.
In this sense all Christian ethics are in fact an " interim
ethic ".

It is just this circumstance that puts faith in

opposition to every other form of life, and constitutes its freedom alike from a realism without principle and from the rigid legality of the idea-worshipper. But here is a point that must least of all be overlooked ; it is that faith is faith no longer when it is confused with the right form of life. In that case the believer ceases to be a pilgrim ; his faith is secularized, either orthodox or clerical, or both together. To have faith —really have it, means to be a man on the watch. For what faith possesses—really possesses—is the promise of that which as yet it does not possess. *Verbum solum habemus.*

INDEX OF AUTHORS' NAMES